The Golf
Geek's Bible

The Golf
Geek's Bible

Rex Hoggard

MQ Publications Ltd

Published by MQ Publications Ltd
12 The Ivories
6–8 Northampton Street
London N1 2HY
Tel: 020 7359 2244
Fax: 020 7359 1616
E-mail: mail@mqpublications.com

North American office
49 West 24th Street
8th Floor
New York, NY 10010
E-mail: information@mqpublicationsus.com

Website: www.mqpublications.com

ISBN: 1-84601-112-4
      978-1-84601-112-2

1 3 5 7 9 0 8 6 4 2

Printed in India

Contents

Introduction

It is a seamless connection to the past that makes golf unlike any other athletic endeavor. Arnold Palmer can recite with perfect clarity playing his first Masters Tournament alongside Ben Hogan and Byron Nelson, legends from a previous generation.

Stand on the first tee at the Old Course in St. Andrews, Scotland, and consider that they were playing the game on the ancient links when man still thought the world was flat.

Golf's timeline stretches back 500 years and weaves a rich tapestry that is unbroken from the days of the "Featherie" golf ball to today's titanium drivers. And so it seemed, this connection from one generation to the next was the best way to tell the story of golf.

I am frequently asked who my favorite players are? It's always a surprise when I admit my dream foursome includes the likes of Jason Gore, Jerry Foltz, Charles Warren, and Joe Ogilvie. The casual golf fan would be pressed to pick any of them out of a lineup, but they are all fine players. More importantly they are thoughtful and genuine people.

They also have the best stories, which is why I've tried to include a healthy mix of tales from these salt-of-the-earth types, along with stories from golf's royalty (Jack Nicklaus, Palmer, Tiger Woods, et al.).

It is by happenstance, not design, that some eras received more attention than others. The 1920s and '30s, for example, were considered the "Golden Age" of golf course architecture and therefore provided more editorial fodder.

No project of this scope is ever accomplished alone and I must thank my wife, Deanne, and Johnny Holder, a childhood friend and regular four-ball partner, for their counsel and encouragement. I'd also like to thank my three boys—Zack, Cole, and Luke—for providing an occasional and much-needed distraction.

Thanks to Catherine Osborne with MQ Publications for her support and patience, and Dave Seanor, my editor at *Golfweek* whose extensive golf library was an invaluable resource.

I also must acknowledge the U.S. Golf Association's Golf House in Far Hills, N.J., and www.usga.org. No other place has captured the rich and varied history of the game like the Golf House. And no other sport invokes such a diverse collection of emotions—triumph, defeat, joy, dejection—like golf.

Enjoy the game.

Contenders & characters

"I never wanted to be a millionaire. I just wanted to live like one."

Walter Hagen

A NEW RECORD ON THE OLD COURSE

In 1858, Allan Robertson, considered golf's first professional, becomes the first player to break 80. He did it on the Old Course at St. Andrews, Scotland.

TRAGEDY FOR YOUNG TOM

Following a match in 1875 at North Berwick, Scotland, Young Tom Morris is informed via telegram his wife of one year is in a grave condition following childbirth. While in transit back to his home in St. Andrews, Young Tom learns that his wife and first child have died. A few months later, on Christmas Day, Young Tom at the age of 24 dies. There was no official cause of death, but legend has long held he died of a broken heart.

Second family of golf

Old and Young Tom Morris are widely considered golf's first family, but the Parks— including Willie Sr., son Willie Jr., and brother Mungo—dominated the professional game in Europe well into the late 19th century. Including the first Open Championship in 1860, Willie Park Sr. was a four-time champion and Mungo won the Open in 1874, the first year it was played at the Park's home course in Musselburgh, Scotland.

DELAYED CROWNING

When is a British Amateur champion not a champion? When he's A. E. MacFie. In 1885, MacFie rolled over Horace Hutchinson, 7 and 6, at Hoylake in England in what was, at the time, simply a gathering of the area's top amateurs. A year later, the Royal and Ancient Golf Club officially dubbed the tournament the British Amateur Championship. It wasn't until 1922, however, that MacFie was recognized as the first British Amateur champion.

An Isle sweep for Adair

Rhona Adair wins the 1900 British Ladies and Irish Ladies championships and wraps up her year by winning a long-drive contest at Royal Lytham and St. Annes with a 173-yard shot.

MACDONALD MAKES HIS POINT

In 1894, C.B. Macdonald finishes runner-up at a tournament called "national amateur championships" at Newport (Rhode Island) Country Club. Macdonald calls for the Amateur Golf Association of the United States—soon to be called the U.S. Golf Association—to universally recognize a single national championship. A year later, Macdonald becomes the winner of the first official U.S. Amateur Championship at Newport.

DELAYED DOMINATION

After scorching the qualifying rounds with a 157 total at the 1901 U.S. Amateur, Walter Travis's march to his second Amateur title is delayed a week because of the death of U.S. President William McKinley. Following the funeral services for the slain leader, Travis defeats Walter Egan, 5 and 4, in the final match.

WESTERN SHOOTER

Willie Anderson becomes the first player to break the 300-mark in a 72-hole tournament played in the United States. Anderson wins the 1902 Western Open with a 299 total.

Sub-80 sensation

Using the recently released "Haskell" ball, Laurie Auchterlonie shoots rounds of 78–78–74–77 at the 1902 U.S. Open to become the first player to card four sub-80 rounds in a single tournament. Auchterlonie wins the championship by six strokes.

HARRIED HARRY

In 1903, at Prestwick in Scotland, Harry Vardon wins his fourth British Open title—a six-stroke romp over his brother Tom. Shortly afterward, Harry Vardon is diagnosed with tuberculosis. Although Vardon would go on to win two more British titles (1911, 1914), he struggles with health problems for the rest of his life.

EAGLE SENDS TRAVIS SOARING

Walter Travis's bid for a fourth U.S. Amateur title is cut short in 1904 when George Ormiston holes his approach shot for an eagle-2 in the second round for a surprising 3-and-1 victory. There was some solace for Travis: later that year he wins the first of three consecutive North & South Amateur titles and co-authors the book *The Art of Putting*.

SISTER ACT

A year after each advanced to the quarterfinals of the U.S. Women's Amateur, Harriot and Margaret Curtis clash in the final match of the 1907 championship. Harriot wins the match, 7 and 6, at Midlothian Country Club in Illinois.

HAVING A BALL

THE 1907 BRITISH AMATEUR ENDS IN A ROUT, WHEN JOHN BALL DOWNS C. A. PALMER, 6 AND 4. THE VICTORY IS BALL'S SIXTH BRITISH AMATEUR TITLE BUT HIS FIRST ON THE HALLOWED LINKS OF THE OLD COURSE AT ST. ANDREWS.

OLD TOM DIES

Thirty-three years after losing his son, Old Tom Morris dies at 86. The four-time British Open champion suffers a concussion after falling down a flight of stairs on May 24, 1908, and never recovers.

Dorothy's double

In what was the early version of the Grand Slam, Britain's Dorothy Campbell wins both the 1909 Ladies' British Open and U.S. Women's Amateur.

PRESIDENTIAL PROWESS

Although he was hardly the only U.S. president with an affinity for golf, William Howard Taft may have been the most passionate about the game. It was said his golf often took precedence over his presidential duties and his ability, other than a questionable short game, was above average.

EVANS UNMATCHED

Charles "Chick" Evans becomes the first amateur to win the Western Open in 1910 and the first champion to prevail under the event's new match-play format.

Hilton's historic sweep

At 42, Harold H. Hilton was hardly the picture of the perfect champion. He used a short-shafted putter that forced him to hunch over to make a stroke and often played a shot with a lit cigarette dangling from his mouth. But in 1911, Hilton won his third consecutive British Amateur at Prestwick and crossed the Atlantic Ocean to claim the U.S. Amateur.

CHICAGO STROLL

Jerome Travers shared medalist honors with Harold Hilton at the 1912 U.S. Amateur but that's as close as he came to being challenged. Travers easily rolled through match play, pounding Chick Evans, 7 and 6, in the final at Chicago Golf Club to take his third Amateur title.

Two of a kind

A year after his stunning victory at the U.S. Open, Francis Ouimet becomes the first player to win both the Open and U.S. Amateur. Ouimet, who also won the French Amateur in May, easily dispatches defending champion Jerome Travers, 6 and 5, in the final of the 1914 U.S. Amateur at Ekwanok Country Club in Vermont.

SIZZLING SWAN SONG

JERRY TRAVERS COMPLETES HIS COMPETITIVE CAREER WITH A VICTORY AT THE 1915 U.S. OPEN AT BALTUSROL GOLF CLUB IN NEW JERSEY. THE SECOND AMATEUR IN THREE YEARS TO WIN THE OPEN AND THE U.S. AMATEUR, HE RETIRES AT 28.

WANAMAKER'S DREAM

On January 17, 1916, wealthy businessman Rodman Wanamaker calls a meeting of the country's golf professionals. For decades, pros had been considered second-class citizens, but Wanamaker persuades them to organize. From that meeting, which is held at the Taplow Club in New York City, the Professional Golfers Association is formed. Wanamaker would later donate the trophy and prize money for the maiden PGA Championship.

Jones's Amateur debut

At 14 years old, Bobby Jones makes his first appearance in the 1916 U.S. Amateur at Merion Cricket Club, losing in the quarterfinals to Bob Gardner, 5 and 3.

A Ray of hope

Often overshadowed by Great Britain's Triumvirate (James Braid, J. H. Taylor, and Harry Vardon), 43-year-old Ted Ray finally seals his place in golf history with his rousing victory at the 1920 U.S. Open. It was Ray's second major title (his first being the 1912 British Open) and came at the expense of an old foe—Vardon, who finishes one shot back.

WHO IS EUGENIO SARACENI?

The Harrison, New York-born pro went on to record 57 victories, including the 1922 U.S. Open and PGA Championship, but he was known throughout his entire adult life as Gene Sarazen. A sixth-grade dropout who grew up in New York City, Sarazen changed his name because "Saraceni sounded more like a violinist than a golfer."

THE ERA OF JONES

Having won his first major championship (the 1923 U.S. Open), perennial runner-up Bobby Jones sets the tone for what becomes one of the most prolific runs in competitive golf with his runaway victory at the 1924 U.S. Amateur. After a half-dozen attempts, Jones sails through match play beating Francis Ouimet, 11 and 10, in the semifinals and George Von Elm, 9 and 8, in the finals.

THE HAIG

Flamboyant and confident, Walter Hagen made a career out of colorful antics on and off the course. Stories abound about "The Haig's" after-hours exploits, many of which seemed to last right through to his morning tee times. More than once Hagen arrived on the first tee wearing a tuxedo rumpled from a night of debauchery. Some say Hagen's "good time" persona was a carefully orchestrated ruse. But one story that is not debated is Hagen's response to the news that his opponent in the final match at the 1926 PGA Championship was home in bed while Hagen was out carousing. "He may be in bed, but he isn't sleeping," said Hagen, referring to the fear he instilled in most of his opponents.

COVER GIRL

Reigning U.S. Women's Amateur champion Edith Cummings becomes the first golfer to be featured on the cover of Time *magazine in 1924.*

ONE-HIT WONDER

For every legend of the game, there are a dozen players who stole the spotlight before fading into obscurity. One of the first one-hit wonders was Willie MacFarlane, who outdueled the greats of the game—Bobby Jones, Francis Ouimet, Gene Sarazen, Walter Hagen—at the 1925 U.S. Open. It was MacFarlane's only major victory.

FAST HARRY

ON HIS WAY TO VICTORY AT THE 1926 LOS ANGELES OPEN, HARRY COOPER IS DUBBED "LIGHTHORSE" BY JOURNALIST DAMON RUNYON FOR HIS FAST PLAY.

"WEE" BOBBY

Although he more resembled a jockey, the undersized Bobby Cruickshank was one of the best players in the late 1920s. During a five-week period in 1927, Cruickshank won three tour events, including the Los Angeles Open.

COLLETT CRUISES

Glenna Collett solidified her hold on the U.S. Women's Amateur title, cruising to victory in the 1928 championship with a 13-and-12 finals trouncing of Virginia Van Wie.

Timeless Tolley

Cyril Tolley—the 1920 British Amateur champion who survived 13 months in a German prison camp during World War I—ends the decade the same way he started it, winning the 1929 British Amateur.

SAVANNAH STUNNER

Horton Smith wins the 1930 Savannah Open and hands Bobby Jones the final loss of his competitive career. As a consolation, Jones is awarded a double-barreled shotgun for being low amateur. Jones also eases the blow of his loss in Savannah with consecutive victories in the U.S. and British Opens and U.S. and British Amateurs.

BURKE NEEDS EXTRA EFFORT

In the longest playoff in U.S. Open history, Billy Burke survives 72 extra holes to claim his first, and only, Open title over George Von Elm in 1931 at the Inverness Club in Ohio. The former iron mill worker is the first Open champion to use steel-shafted clubs.

VARDON'S FAREWELL

In his last round of championship golf, just two spectators watch Harry Vardon's attempt to qualify for the 1932 British Open. The six-time Open champion struggles to a round in the "high 80s" and fails to advance to the championship.

OH, CANADA

C. Ross "Sandy" Somerville becomes the
first Canadian to win the U.S. Amateur in 1932.
Somerville, a six-time Canadian Amateur champion,
edged Johnny Goodman, 2 and 1, in the final match.

ALWAYS A BRIDESMAID

*Maureen Orcutt was a regular contender among
the women's amateur ranks, but she was never
able to reach the winner's circle. One of her
closest near misses came at the 1933 U.S.
Women's Amateur, where she lost in the
semifinals to Virginia Van Wie. Orcutt eventually
gave up competitive golf to pursue her second
calling, as a golf writer for* The New York Times.

CLASS ACT

Englishman Henry Cotton was something of a
visionary in his day. The 1934 British Open champion
was the first pro to emerge from the upper class but
he stunned his family when he left school at age 17
to become a professional golfer.

"LITTLE SLAM"

LAWSON LITTLE, THE LONG-HITTING SON OF A U.S. ARMY
OFFICER, EASILY WINS THE 1934 U.S. AND BRITISH
AMATEURS TO COMPLETE WHAT IS CALLED THE "LITTLE
SLAM." LITTLE WOULD MATCH THE ACCOMPLISHMENT
AGAIN IN 1935 AND IN 1936.

RUNYAN CASHES IN

In 1934, the PGA Tour's first official season, Paul Runyan wins six times and earns $6,767 to become the circuit's leading money winner.

WHAT'S IN A NAME?

Prescott S. Bush is named president of the U.S. Golf Association in 1934. Bush's maternal grandfather, George Herbert Walker, held the same post in 1920. The family's stock continues to rise, however, when Bush's son, George, becomes the United States' 41st president in 1989 and is followed to the White House by grandson George W. Bush.

FINAL GASP FOR HAGEN

At 42 years old, Walter Hagen finishes his final round with back-to-back birdies to win the 1935 Gasparilla Open in Tampa, Florida. The triumph marks Hagen's final victory in an individual tournament.

BERG'S BIG YEAR

Freckle-faced and aggressive, Patty Berg emerges as the next great women's champion. In 1936, Berg wins the Florida Women's Amateur and helps the U.S. Curtis Cup team play the Great Britain and Ireland side to a draw. She also shuns traditional golf attire for more comfortable and functional garb.

BYRD IN FLIGHT

Sam Byrd, who replaced Babe Ruth in right field for the New York Yankees, wins the little-known Baseball Players Tournament in 1937. Following his baseball career, Byrd becomes a two-time PGA Tour winner.

LADIES FIRST

Babe Didrikson becomes the first woman to play a PGA Tour event. Didrikson—who earned her spot in the tournament via a 36-hole qualifier—cards rounds of 76–81–79 and fails to advance to the final round at the 1938 Los Angeles Open. On top of her historic achievement, Didrikson also scored a personal victory. She met her future husband, George Zaharias, at the event.

DAPPER DEMARET

Jimmy Demaret wins his first PGA Tour event, the 1938 San Francisco Match Play, and quickly makes a name for himself as a stylish trendsetter. Demaret, who would occasionally moonlight as a nightclub singer, has an affinity for brightly colored clothes and peculiar hats.

ARMOUR FINALÉ

Tommy Armour wins the 1938 Mid-South Open, the final PGA Tour title in his distinguished career.

FIRST TO 59

Harold McSpaden is the first to shoot 59 during a practice round for the 1939 Texas Open at Brackenridge Park in San Antonio. Although he follows his phenomenal round with a 63 during the tournament, E. J. Harrison takes the title.

PATTY JOINS PAY-FOR-PLAY RANKS

After 29 amateur victories, Patty Berg turns professional. Because there are few women's pro events in 1940, she spends most of her time giving exhibitions and clinics.

FEELING THE DRAFT

In 1942, Sam Snead is granted a 10-day extension to play the PGA Championship before having to report for induction into the U.S. Navy. Slammin' Sammy made the most of the extension, beating Jim Turnesa, 2 and 1, in the finals to claim his first major title. The next day, Snead reported for duty.

ALL HALE HOGAN

BEN HOGAN WINS THE 1942 HALE AMERICA NATIONAL OPEN AT RIDGEMOOR COUNTRY CLUB IN CHICAGO—A SCALED-DOWN VERSION OF THE U.S. OPEN, WHICH IS SPONSORED BY THE USGA.

GRANDFATHER CLOCKS NORTH & SOUTH FIELD

With most players overseas fighting in World War II, the 1943 North & South Open is limited to players 38 or older. Bobby Cruickshank, a 48-year-old grandfather, wins.

THE STREAK

Byron Nelson begins his unprecedented victory romp in 1945 with a team triumph at the Miami Four-Ball and closes out his 11-event title sweep in August at the Canadian Open. Along the way, Nelson wins his second PGA Championship. He finishes the season with 18 total victories and more than $60,000 in war bonds. He retires after the 1946 season at the age of 34.

GEORGE THE GREAT

Before he became one of the game's most insightful golf course architects, George Fazio pieced together a decent career on the PGA Tour. Fazio, who sold cars to pay his way on Tour, won the 1945 California State Open and the 1946 Canadian Open.

THREE AND OUT

Although he'd win 13 events and over $40,000, 1946 is remembered as the year Ben Hogan let two major titles slip away. At Augusta National, Hogan three-putted from 12 feet on the final hole to finish a shot behind Herman Keiser. Another three-putt on the 72nd hole of the U.S. Open again cost him. At the PGA in Oregon, Hogan earns some redemption with his 6-and-4 finals victory over Ed Oliver.

"MISS SLUGGS"

Amateur Louise Suggs, nicknamed "Miss Sluggs" for her booming drives, overpowers her professional competitors to win the 1946 Titleholders tournament and Women's Western Open.

A QUICK SMILE

Despite his extra-hole loss to Stanley Bishop at the 1946 U.S. Amateur, Smiley Quick did have one of the best names in the game. Earlier in the year, Quick added his unique moniker to the USGA record books with his victory at the U.S. Amateur Public Links.

Curtis makes golden return

Fifty years after playing in her first U.S. Women's Amateur, Margaret Curtis plays in the 1947 championship. The three-time Women's Amateur champion is 63.

UN-LOCKE A LEGEND

Dubbed "Muffin Face" by his fellow pros, South African Bobby Locke was something of a curiosity when he arrived in the United States in 1947 to play the PGA Tour. He'd soundly beaten Sam Snead during an exhibition years before in South Africa, but no one was prepared for what unfolded. In 1947, Locke—whose less-than-flattering nickname was the result of his rotund features and stoic demeanor—won six events and was narrowly edged by Jimmy Demaret for the money title.

TOUR UNDER SIEGE

The PGA Tour's Caucasian-only clause is challenged by African-American pros Ted Rhodes, Bill Spiller, and Madison Gunter. The trio sue the Tour when they're barred from playing the 1948 Richmond Open in California. In September, the group drops the suit when the Tour promises that no players will be barred from open events because of color.

BERG AND ZAHARIAS LIGHT LPGA FIRE

In January 1948, Patty Berg and Babe Zaharias, two of the game's top players and members of the floundering Women's Professional Golf Association, meet in a Miami hotel to map out the course of a new women's tour. Two years later, the LPGA is formed.

A DARK DAY

On February 2, 1949, Ben Hogan's car collides with a bus outside the small town of Van Horn, Texas. Hogan suffers a fractured collar bone, fractured rib, two cracked bones in his left ankle and two pelvis fractures. A month later, Hogan is flown to El Paso, Texas, for emergency surgery to remove blood clots. Although his career was far from over, the injuries to his legs would keep Hogan from ever playing another PGA Championship, which was a match-play event and particularly exhausting.

LOCKE SNUBBED

The PGA Tour bans Bobby Locke from playing the circuit in 1949 because the South African remains in Britain to play a series of exhibitions instead of honoring his commitment to play in the United States. The Tour lifts the ban two years later.

NO PALOOKA

Joe Kirkwood Jr., the actor-turned-golf-pro who played the lead role in the television series "Joe Palooka," wins the 1949 Philadelphia Inquirer Invitational.

A RIPPLE FROM WAKE

In a prelude to what becomes a Hall of Fame career, 19-year-old Arnold Palmer of Wake Forest takes medalist honors at the 1949 NCAA Championship.

MERION MISFORTUNES

Unheralded Lee Mackey, a former U.S. Army private, sails to an opening-round 64 on the demanding East Course at Merion Golf Club at the 1950 U.S. Open. Mackey follows his tournament-record round with a sloppy 81 in Round 2.

TRAGIC END FOR TRAVERS

On March 30, 1951, Jerome D. Travers dies a pauper at 64. A life-time amateur who won the 1915 U.S. Open and four U.S. Amateur titles, he struggled financially for most of his life. In 1938, he sold one of his famous golf clubs to feed his family.

WRONG NUMBER

Following a third-round 62 at the 1951 St. Paul Open, Lloyd Mangrum receives a midnight telephone call saying that if he wins the event, he won't leave town alive. The next day, with police protection, Mangrum shoots 70 and wins by a stroke without incident.

BE LIKE "IKE"

Although hampered by a knee injury sustained while playing football for West Point, Dwight D. Eisenhower's passion for golf was legendary and it helped spark a postwar golf boom in the United States. After being elected president in 1952, "Ike" had a putting green installed behind the White House, and a cabin he would stay in at Augusta National Golf Club, where he was a member, was dubbed the "Little White House."

A TRUE OPEN

Taking advantage of a new PGA Tour rule that allows African-American players to compete in a tournament as long as the event's sponsor agrees, Ted Rhodes, Bill Spiller, and amateur Eural Clark play the 1952 Phoenix Open.

WAIT OVER FOR WESTLAND

In 1952, at Seattle Golf Club, Jack Westland downs Al Mengert, 3 and 2, in the final match to win the U.S. Amateur. Westland—who finished runner-up to Francis Ouimet in the 1931 Amateur—has history on his side. At 47, he becomes the championship's oldest winner.

"TERRIBLE TOMMY"

Tommy Bolt wins the 1953 Tucson Open to build on a budding career, but it's Bolt's temper that people are noticing. Christened "Terrible Tommy" for his temper tantrums, Bolt breaks two golf clubs and tosses a third club in the water on his way to a second-round 81 at the Colonial Invitational later that year.

SURGERY SLOWS BABE

Days after winning the 1953 Babe Didrikson Zaharias Open in her hometown of Beaumont, Texas, Babe Didrikson undergoes surgery for colon cancer. After being stricken with cancer for the second time in 1956, she dies on September 27. The three-time Women's Open champion and Olympic gold medalist is only 42.

EASY MONEY

A trio of top pros—including defending champion Lloyd Mangrum, Cary Middlecoff, and Jack Burke—withdraw from the 1953 Pan American Open in Mexico City after they learn Ben Hogan receives a $5,000 guarantee to play in the event. Hogan easily wins the tournament.

A KING COMING INTO HIS OWN

Charismatic and daring, 24-year-old Arnold Palmer beats Robert Sweeny on the final hole of the 1954 U.S. Amateur. Moments after Palmer's winning putt drops, a brass band plays "Hail to the Chief."

WORTH THE WAIT

Barbara Romack wins the 1954 U.S. Women's Amateur, ousting Mickey Wright, 4 and 2, in a final match that was delayed 29 hours and 15 minutes because of thunderstorms.

GOLF'S $50,000 MAN

Bob Toski squeaks out a one-stroke victory at the 1954 George S. May's World Championship and earns $50,000, at the time golf's biggest purse.

BAD DAY FOR CRIME BOSS

Anthony Capezio, a well-known member of a Chicago organized crime family who had an affinity for golf, dies July 7, 1955, of a heart attack while playing a round at White Pines Country Club near Chicago.

ARNIE'S FIRST PAYDAY

ARNOLD PALMER WINS THE 1955 CANADIAN OPEN FOR HIS FIRST PROFESSIONAL TITLE.

AN OPEN FIRST

Ann Gregory becomes the first African-American woman to play in an USGA tournament when she tees off in the 1956 U.S. Women's Open.

GOING IN THE TANK

Don January, George Bayer, and Ernie Vossler are suspended by the PGA Tour for 30 days after deliberately shooting high scores in the third round of the 1957 Kentucky Derby Open. The group was irate that they'd not been allowed to withdraw from the event after making the cut.

TRAILBLAZER

Charlie Sifford wins the 1957 Long Beach Open to become the first African-American to win an event sanctioned by the PGA Tour.

TWO-HORSE RACE

Overshadowed by Arnold Palmer's victory at the Masters 14 days earlier, diminutive Gary Player wins the 1958 Kentucky Derby Open. The 22-year-old South African will become Palmer's primary rival.

A LIGHT FOR THE LPGA

QUIET AND UNASSUMING, BETSY RAWLS'S HERCULEAN EFFORT IN 1959 GAVE THE STRUGGLING LPGA TOUR A NEEDED BOOST. RAWLS WON 10 TITLES—OR NEARLY 40 PERCENT OF THE LPGA'S 26 EVENTS—INCLUDING THE LPGA CHAMPIONSHIP AND WOMEN'S WESTERN OPEN.

OHIO ACE

A 19 year old from Columbus, Ohio, arrives at the Broadmoor Golf Club in Colorado for the 1959 U.S. Amateur as a little-known collegian. By the time Jack Nicklaus is finished, he's dethroned defending champion Charles Coe, 1 up, in the final match and won the first of what will be many championships.

ALL THE WRIGHT MOVES

Bill Wright becomes the first African-American to win a USGA event when he defeats Frank H. Campbell, 3 and 2, in the final of the 1959 U.S. Amateur Public Links.

A FAMILY AFFAIR

Jay Hebert narrowly defeats Jim Ferrier to win the 1960 PGA Championship. Hebert and his brother, Lionel, who won the 1957 PGA, are the only brothers to win the Wanamaker Trophy.

STILL SLAMMING

Timeless Sam Snead, 49, wins the 1961 Tournament of Champions in Las Vegas. It's "The Slammer's" 80th career victory and pays the winner 10,000 silver dollars.

PEBBLE BEACH POUNDING

In one of the most lopsided finals victories at the U.S. Amateur, Jack Nicklaus hammers H. Dudley Wysong Jr., 8 and 6, to win the 1961 championship on the storied links at Pebble Beach.

AGELESS EVANS

CHICK EVANS BECOMES THE FIRST PLAYER TO COMPETE IN 50 U.S. AMATEURS WHEN HE TEES IT UP AT THE 1962 CHAMPIONSHIP AT THE AGE OF 72.

 THE GOLF GEEK'S BIBLE

"FAT JACK"

Jack Nicklaus may have been the first pro to embrace the fitness craze. When he first joined the PGA Tour in 1962 he was so overweight he was dubbed "Fat Jack" by his fellow players and fans. Before his Hall of Fame career was over, however, he'd shed his less-flattering moniker for a more endearing nickname—"Golden Bear."

GETTING IT RIGHT

Jay Hebert leads a threat by players to boycott the 1964 Phoenix Open in a dispute over television rights. Tournament organizers and the players reach a compromise and the tournament is played.

SURGERIES SIDELINE VENTURI

Less than a year after his breakthrough victory in the 1964 U.S. Open, Ken Venturi undergoes two surgeries to correct a circulation problem in his right hand. He returned to the PGA Tour in 1966, winning the Luck International Open in January. It was his last Tour victory.

GREENSBORO GRAND FOR SAMMY

With a putt so long Sam Snead said it was "from China to Japan," Slammin' Sammy scored a victory for older players at the 1965 Greater Greensboro Open. The birdie at No. 13 during the final round gave Snead a lead he wouldn't relinquish on his way to a five-stroke victory. At 52 years, 10 months, Snead becomes the PGA Tour's oldest winner and claims his eighth Greensboro crown.

BUFFALO BILLY

Billy Casper loses 40 pounds on an exotic diet that includes avocado pears and buffalo meat and wins the 1965 Western Open with a final-round 64.

LEMA'S LEGACY CUT SHORT

Tony Lema and his wife, Betty, are killed in 1966 when the private plane they are on crashes into the seventh hole of The Sportsman's Club in Lansing, Michigan. Lema was traveling from the PGA Championship to an exhibition in Chicago.

LONG HAUL

JOANNE GUNDERSON CARNER WINS THE 1966 U.S. WOMEN'S AMATEUR BUT SHE NEEDS 41 HOLES TO EDGE MARLENE STEWART. IT'S THE LONGEST MATCH IN CHAMPIONSHIP HISTORY.

FLECKMAN THE FLASH

One of the games great flash-in-the-pans, Marty Fleckman emerges in 1967 when he leads the U.S. Open as an amateur through 54 holes. Fleckman fades with a closing 80 but follows with a victory later that year at the Cajun Classic in Louisiana, the first tournament he enters as a pro. It is Fleckman's only Tour victory.

SECOND STINGS NICKLAUS

IN A RARE OFF-YEAR, JACK NICKLAUS FINISHES RUNNER-UP AT THE 1968 BRITISH OPEN, AND THE SAME AT THE U.S. OPEN AND TWO SHOTS BEHIND CANADIAN OPEN WINNER BOB CHARLES.

WHEN A WIN'S NOT A WIN

Tommy Aaron clips Sam Snead in a playoff at the 1969 Canadian Open. He's still winless on the PGA Tour because the event is considered unofficial.

TAPPED OUT

Larry Ziegler wins the 1969 Michigan Golf Classic but quickly learns officials don't have the money to pay out the $100,000 purse.

HAGEN MOURNED
On October 6, 1969, Walter Hagen dies of throat cancer. He is 76. Arnold Palmer serves as a pallbearer at the funeral in Birmingham, Michigan.

OCCUPATIONAL HAZARD
During the pro-am portion of the 1970 Bob Hope Desert Classic, U.S. Vice President Spiro Agnew badly shanks a 3-wood and hits pro partner Doug Sanders on the head with a wayward tee shot. Sanders is uninjured.

MOON BALL
Using the head of a Spalding 6-iron—which he'd hidden onboard the Apollo 14 spacecraft—attached to a tool used to scoop up lunar soil, astronaut Alan Shepard becomes the first human to hit a golf shot on the moon, in February 1971.

TEXAS TWO-STEP
BEN CRENSHAW BECOMES THE FIRST FRESHMAN TO WIN THE NCAA CHAMPIONSHIP INDIVIDUAL CROWN IN 1971, AND HE LEADS THE UNIVERSITY OF TEXAS TO THE TEAM TITLE.

GOLF LOSES A LEGEND

After years of suffering from a crippling spinal ailment, Bobby Jones dies on December 18, 1971. Jones, the winner of 13 major championships and the co-founder of Augusta National Golf Club, is 69.

55 THE LIMIT FOR RAWLS

BETSY RAWLS WINS THE 1972 GAC CLASSIC. IT'S HER 55TH AND FINAL LPGA VICTORY.

Brewer bounces back

After suffering a near-fatal ulcer on the eve of the 1972 Masters, Gay Brewer, 40, recovers to win that year's Canadian Open and the Ben Hogan Award for his "courage in the face of trying circumstances."

ONE SIZZLING SUMMER

A middle-of-the-road pro with five PGA Tour victories, Tom Weiskopf came to life in the summer of 1973. Following three Tour triumphs (Colonial, Kemper Open, and Philadelphia Classic), Weiskopf claims his only major at the British Open in Troon, Scotland. He wraps up his year with No. 5 at the Canadian Open.

"THE KING'S" CLOSING

In 1972, Arnold Palmer fails to win a Tour event for the first time in 17 years. He returns to the winner's circle at the 1973 Bob Hope Desert Classic, but this is to be the last PGA Tour victory of "The King's" 60-win career.

BEN AT HIS BEST

PLAYING HIS FIRST EVENT AS A PRO, BEN CRENSHAW CLOSES WITH 66 TO WIN THE 1973 SAN ANTONIO TEXAS OPEN.

FAST STARTER

Johnny Miller kicks off his stellar year with early-season victories at the 1974 Bing Crosby National Pro-Am, Phoenix Open, and Tucson Open. He opens his season with 24 consecutive rounds of par or better.

DEANE OF THE PGA TOUR

After a decent playing career, Deane Beman retires in 1974 to take over the job of PGA Tour commissioner from Joseph Dey. Beman's reign as Tour chief lasts 20 years.

ELDER STATESMAN
Lee Elder wins the 1974 Monsanto Open to become the first African-American to earn an invitation to the Masters.

A bolt out of the blue
Lee Trevino, Bobby Nichols, and Jerry Heard are hospitalized after being hit by lightning during the second round of the 1975 Western Open. Hale Irwin wins the event by a stroke.

ROOKIE MISTAKE
In his first year on the PGA Tour, Roger Maltbie wins the 1975 Quad Cities Open and Pleasant Valley Classic, where he makes the biggest mistake of his young career. Maltbie leaves his $40,000 winner's check in a restaurant near the course. Officials give him another check.

MR. 59
With a scorching round that includes a stretch of seven holes he plays in 8 under par, Al Geiberger becomes the first to shoot 59 in a PGA Tour event at the 1977 Danny Thomas Memphis Classic. Geiberger caps his historic feat with an 8-foot birdie putt at the last hole to set up a three-shot victory.

TOM TERRIFIC

In 1977, Tom Watson emerges as the game's next great player. Watson tops Jack Nicklaus by two shots to win the Masters, and he birdies the last hole to edge the "Golden Bear" again at the British Open. In total, Watson wins four times in 1977 and is named the PGA Tour's player of the year.

Tragedy at Augusta National

Augusta National co-founder and former club chairman Clifford Robert dies in September 1977 of an apparent self-inflicted gunshot wound on club grounds.

DIVINE NINE FOR LOPEZ

In her first year on the LPGA, 21-year-old Nancy Lopez is nearly unstoppable. She wins nine times in 1978—including the LPGA Championship—and collects the tour's rookie and player of the year honors as well as a record $189,813 in earnings.

SCRAMBLING SEVE

Spain's Seve Ballesteros wins the 1978 Greater Greensboro Open and quickly makes a name for himself with his ability to recover from bad shots. As one journalist notes: "He can get up-and-down from a parking lot."

ACTING HIS AGE

Sam Snead, 67, becomes the first player to shoot his age in a PGA Tour event at the 1979 Quad Cities Open. He follows his second-round 67 with a closing 66.

A sportsman's salute

Jack Nicklaus's domination of golf in the 1970s helps golf blossom into a mainstream sport, as evidenced by *Sports Illustrated* magazine naming "The Golden Bear" its Sportsman of the Decade in 1980. He punctuates this honor by winning that year's U.S. Open and PGA Championship at the age of 40.

FUN AND FAIRWAYS

Comedians Bill Murray, Chevy Chase, Ted Knight, and Rodney Dangerfield team up in the 1980 movie Caddyshack. *Though the plot is flimsy, the movie becomes a cult classic for golfers and non-golfers alike.*

AROUND THE WORLD IN FOUR MONTHS

A respected putter with a thin résumé, Bill Rogers came to life in 1981—winning seven tournaments around the globe, including six victories in a four-month span. Rogers won three times on the PGA Tour, twice in Australia, and once in Japan. But the highlight of his year came in July, when he won the British Open at Royal St. George's in England. In 1989, however, after a barren stretch that included just one victory, Rogers quit the Tour and became a club professional.

A CROSBY CHAMPION

Nathaniel Crosby, the son of crooner Bing, wins the 1981 U.S. Amateur. The event is played at Olympic Country Club in San Francisco, about 15 miles from the Crosby home.

PATE MAKES A SPLASH

Jerry Pate wins the 1982 Tournament Players Championship, the first played at the new TPC at Sawgrass in Florida. To celebrate, Pate pushes PGA Tour commissioner Deane Beman and Sawgrass designer Pete Dye into the pond adjacent the 18th green before jumping in behind them. So confident was Pate that he would win, he announced the prank while still playing the 72nd hole. "I hadn't even won the tournament yet. I looked right at the camera and said, 'Pete Dye will go for a swim today,'" Pate said.

WHITWORTH SCORES 83RD IN '82
Kathy Whitworth wins the 1982 Lady Michelob to claim her 83rd career victory and eclipse Mickey Wright's record of 82. Whitworth will finish her career with 88 titles.

DAY AT THE BEACH
Hale Irwin's tee shot on the scenic 18th hole at Pebble Beach Golf Links during the 1983 National Pro-Am hooks badly toward the beach, caroms off a rock and back onto the fairway. Irwin birdies the hole and beats Jim Nelford in a playoff.

FORMIDABLE FIRSTS
NICK FALDO (HERITAGE CLASSIC) AND GREG NORMAN (KEMPER OPEN) WIN THEIR FIRST PGA TOUR EVENTS WITHIN THREE MONTHS OF EACH OTHER IN 1984.

ZOELLER BACK IN ACTION
Six months after undergoing surgery to repair ruptured discs in his back, Fuzzy Zoeller wins the 1985 Bay Hill Classic by two strokes.

CHIP OFF THE GOLDEN BLOCK

Jack Nicklaus Jr. wins the 1985 North & South Amateur. Nicklaus's famous father, Jack Sr., won the event in 1959.

MAC THE KNIFE

Mac O'Grady calls PGA Tour commissioner Deane Beman "little Hitler" and a "thief with a capital T" after he's fined $500 for a 1984 incident. Beman suspends O'Grady for six weeks for his comments.

It's only money

Payne Stewart finishes with a tournament-record 264 total to win the 1987 Bay Hill Classic. The central Florida resident donates the $108,000 winner's check to the Florida Hospital Cancer Center.

CAR TROUBLE

Jan Stephenson shares the 54-hole lead at the 1987 S&H Classic, but is injured in a car accident and can't play the final round. Less than two months later, Stephenson recovers and wins the Safeco Classic.

LIFE SAVER

Playing in a qualifying tournament for the 1988 Standard Register Turquoise Classic, Mary Bea Porter saves the life of a young boy who nearly drowns in a swimming pool adjacent the golf course.

LOVE JR. DIES IN PLANE CRASH

DAVIS LOVE JR., RENOWNED GOLF INSTRUCTOR AND FATHER OF FUTURE PGA TOUR STAR DAVIS LOVE III, DIES IN A PLANE CRASH IN NOVEMBER 1988.

A PURE PUTTER

Considered one of the PGA Tour's top putters, Kenny Knox sets the record for fewest putts in a 72-hole tournament at the 1989 MCI Heritage Classic. Knox needs just 93 putts on Harbour Town Golf Links' small greens.

DELIGHTFUL DEBUT

PGA Tour rookie Robert Gamez wins his first event, the 1990 Northern Telecom Tucson Open, and adds another title to his résumé—the Nestle Invitational—two months later, when he holes his 7-iron approach on the 72nd hole for eagle.

FANTASTIC PHIL

Amateur Phil Mickelson wins the 1991 Northern Telecom Open. A year earlier, the left-hander from Arizona State University became the first player since Jack Nicklaus to win the NCAA individual title and the U.S. Amateur in the same year.

GOING LOW

Chip Beck becomes the second player in PGA Tour history to shoot 59 in competition. He accomplishes the feat in the third round of the 1991 Las Vegas Invitational. He doesn't win. That honor went to Andrew Magee, who beat D.A. Weibring in a playoff after both finished with a 90-hole Tour record 31 under par total.

"BOOM BOOM'S" BEST

In one of the fastest starts in PGA Tour history, Fred "Boom Boom" Couples wins the 1992 Los Angeles Open in a playoff, finishes runner-up at the Doral Ryder Open and Honda Open, and slams the field at the Nestle Invitational by nine strokes. He caps his inspiring spring with his first major title at the Masters.

A TIGER NAMED ELDRICK

Eldrick "Tiger" Woods becomes the first player to win the U.S. Junior Amateur three consecutive times in 1993 at Waverley Country Club in Oregon. Three years later, Woods makes more USGA history with his third consecutive U.S. Amateur victory, which also comes in Oregon.

Here's Johnny

Johnny Miller comes out of semi-retirement to win the 1994 AT&T Pebble Beach National Pro-Am by one stroke. It's the 46 year old's 25th and final PGA Tour title.

MEET THE NEW BOSS

TIM FINCHEM, A FORMER LAWYER AND ECONOMIC ADVISOR TO PRESIDENT JIMMY CARTER IN 1978 AND '79, TAKES OVER AS COMMISSIONER OF THE PGA TOUR IN 1994. HE REPLACES DEANE BEMAN WHO HELD THE JOB FOR 20 YEARS.

WRIGHT AND WRONG

In a 1995 interview with the *Wilmington* (Delaware) *News Journal*, CBS broadcaster Ben Wright is quoted as saying, "lesbians in the sport hurt women's golf." Wright claims he was misquoted and CBS initially stands by him, signing Wright to a new, four-year contract. But the uproar over his comments continues, and the network dismisses him in early 1996.

TIGER UNLEASHED

Tiger Woods wins an unprecedented third consecutive U.S. Amateur in a 38-hole shootout in August 1996. Two days later, he turns pro and signs multi-year endorsement deals worth an estimated $60 million. The 20-year-old wunderkind makes an immediate impact on the PGA Tour, winning twice (Las Vegas Invitational, Walt Disney World Classic), qualifying for the Tour Championship, and claiming the circuit's rookie of the year award.

KELLI COMES ALIVE

Although overshadowed by Tiger Woods's pro debut, Kelli Kuehne wins the 1996 U.S. Women's Amateur and the British Ladies Amateur.

THE PRINCE OF PEBBLE

Mark O'Meara wins the 1997 AT&T Pebble Beach Pro-Am, his fifth victory in the event. The triumph foreshadows O'Meara's biggest year on Tour when he'll win the 1998 Masters and British Open.

FUZZY'S FOLLY

A furor erupts after Fuzzy Zoeller, one of the games most engaging and endearing players, makes racially insensitive remarks following Tiger Woods's victory at the 1997 Masters.

LIKE FATHER, LIKE SON

David Duval shoots 59 in the final round of the 1999 Bob Hope Chrysler Classic to win by one shot. A few weeks later, Duval wins The Players Championship the same week his father, Bob, claims his first Senior PGA Tour title, the Emerald Coast Classic.

GOLF WORLD FEELS THE PAYNE

A LearJet carrying reigning U.S. Open champion Payne Stewart and four other people crashes into a South Dakota field on October 25, 1999. Earlier in the day, the LearJet left Orlando, Florida, bound for Dallas, but shortly after takeoff the plane lost cabin pressure, incapacitating the crew and passengers.

SHIGEKI STILL SMILING

JAPAN'S SHIGEKI MARUYAMA, NICKNAMED THE "SMILING ASSASSIN," SHOOTS 58 IN SECTIONAL QUALIFYING FOR THE 2000 U.S. OPEN. MARUYAMA'S ROUND AT WOODMONT COUNTRY CLUB IN ROCKVILLE, MARYLAND, INCLUDES 11 BIRDIES AND AN EAGLE.

WIE WOWS PUBLINKS

Ten-year-old phenom Michelle Wie qualifies for the 2000 U.S. Women's Amateur Public Links Championship, becoming the youngest competitor in a USGA championship. Three years later, Wie wins the event and becomes the youngest champion of an adult USGA championship.

MRS. 59

ANNIKA SÖRENSTAM SHOOTS 59 TO WIN THE 2001 LPGA STANDARD REGISTER PING AND RECORDS THE CIRCUIT'S FIRST SUB-60 ROUND.

A SEMPLE GAME

Life-long amateur Carol Semple Thompson wins the 2002 USGA Senior Women's Amateur for the fourth time. The victory is Semple Thompson's seventh USGA title, putting her two championships behind Bobby Jones's all-time mark of nine. She also establishes a consecutive match-play winning streak of 24 matches.

LEARNING EXPERIENCE

Annika Sörenstam becomes the first woman to play a PGA Tour event since Babe Didrikson Zaharias in 1945. Although she misses the cut at the 2003 Colonial in Texas, Sörenstam continues to dominate the LPGA and credits her experiences at the Colonial for her improvement.

A SURPRISE-SINGH TURN

Since he joined the PGA Tour in 1996, Tiger Woods's dominance was almost unchallenged. That is until 2004. Vijay Singh wins nine times in 2004—including an eight-event stretch that includes six trips to the winner's circle—earns over $10 million, and unseats Woods as the top-ranked player.

Moore magic

Ryan Moore pieces together the best season by an amateur since Bobby Jones won the Grand Slam in 1930, with victories at the U.S. Amateur, U.S. Public Links, NCAA Championship, and Western Amateur in 2004.

GORE DETAILS

Dubbed the smiling "Prince of Pinehurst," pro journeyman Jason Gore begins the final round of the 2005 U.S. Open within three shots of the lead. In the final round, he balloons to a final-round 84 to finish 49th. He recovers with three victories on the secondary Nationwide Tour to regain his playing status on the PGA Tour. A few weeks later, he wins his first PGA Tour event to complete his inspiring comeback.

Grand Slam

"Golf is a game that is played on a five-inch course—the distance between your ears."
Bobby Jones

AN OPEN CHAMPION

Willie Park Sr. wins the first British Open Championship in 1860 over Old Tom Morris on the quirky links at Prestwick in Scotland. Only eight professionals, who at that time were not as highly regarded as the amateurs who played the game, participated and the event featured three rounds of 12 holes.

PARK'S PLACE

Willie Park Sr. wins his second Open title in 1863, again defeating Old Tom Morris by two strokes. Although this is the first year prize money is awarded at the British Open, only the second-, third-, and fourth-place finishers receive cash awards. Park also is given the "championship belt" to keep for one year.

STRATH STUNS OPEN ESTABLISHMENT

Andrew Strath unseats Willie Park and Old Tom Morris, who combined to win the first five championships, at the 1865 British Open. Strath upsets Park by two shots but never contends for the title again.

YOUTH IS SERVED

A year after his father, legendary St. Andrews professional Old Tom Morris, wins the last of his four Open Championship titles, Young Tom Morris claims his first in 1868 at Prestwick. Young Tom, 17, edged Robert Andrew by two shots to become the championship's youngest winner.

TRYING TO YOUNG TOM-PROOF THE OPEN CHAMPIONSHIP

So concerned are they at Young Tom Morris's domination of the British Open (the Scot had won three in a row by a total of 17 strokes), officials cancel the event in 1871 and devise a three-course rotation. To the R&A's chagrin, Young Tom continues his winning ways, cruising to a three-stroke victory in 1872 over David Strath at Prestwick.

A NEW CROWN

Tom Kidd narrowly defeats Jamie Anderson to win the first Open Championship played on the Old Course at St. Andrews in 1873. Kidd, whose 179 total was the highest winning score in the event's 13-year history, also became the first player awarded the silver Claret Jug. Prior champions had received the "championship belt" for one year but it was given permanently to Young Tom Morris in 1872 after he won his fourth consecutive Open.

ANOTHER OPEN EMERGES

England's Horace Rawlins pieces together rounds of 91–82 at Newport (Rhode Island) Golf Club, to win the maiden U.S. Open in 1895. Rawlins, who was a 21-year-old assistant pro at Newport, beat Willie Dunn and nine other contenders to claim the $150 first-place prize.

MUIRFIELD MIGHT

JAMES BRAID WINS THE 1901 BRITISH OPEN AT MUIRFIELD TO BECOME THE FIRST HOMEBRED OPEN CHAMPION SINCE 1893. THE VICTORY IS THE FIRST OF FIVE OPEN CHAMPIONSHIPS FOR BRAID, WHO OUTDUELS REGULAR FOES HARRY VARDON AND J. H. TAYLOR.

A RUNNER-UP RECORD

Although he finishes second, a shot behind champion Jack White, J. H. Taylor's closing-round 68 at the 1904 British Open sets a single-round tournament record that stands for 30 years.

WILLIE SCORES

Willie Anderson solidifies his hold on the U.S. Open record books with his 1905 victory at the Myopia Hunt Club in Illinois. Anderson's two-shot triumph is his fourth Open title and third consecutive. It's a mark that won't be touched until Bobby Jones arrives as an Open champion in the late 1920s. Unfortunately for Anderson, it's also the last time he seriously contends for an Open championship.

SMITH SHEDS BRIDESMAID BLUES

Runner-up at the 1898, 1901, and 1905 U.S. Opens, Alex Smith breaks his string of second-place finishes with his wire-to-wire victory at the 1906 U.S. Open. His 295 total is seven shots better than his nearest competitor, his brother Willie, and marks the first time a player cracks the 300 plateau in either the U.S. or British Opens.

WIN, PLACE, AND SHOW

AT THE 1906 BRITISH OPEN AT MUIRFIELD, THE GREAT TRIUMVIRATE (JAMES BRAID, J. H. TAYLOR, AND HARRY VARDON) SWEEP THE TOP THREE SPOTS, WITH BRAID TAKING THE TITLE OVER SECOND-PLACE TAYLOR AND THIRD-PLACE VARDON.

AN OPENING ACE

Anchored atop the leaderboard through 54 holes at the 1907 U.S. Open, Jack Hobens tumbles from contention with a closing 85 to finish well behind winner Alex Ross. Hobens can take some solace, however, when he records the first hole-in-one in tournament history at the 147-yard 10th hole at Philadelphia Cricket Club in Pennsylvania.

WISPY WINNER

AT A GAUNT 108 POUNDS, FRED MCLEOD MATCHES WILLIE SMITH'S 322 TOTAL AT THE 1908 U.S. OPEN AND TAKES THE TITLE IN A PLAYOFF, EDGING SMITH 77–83 AT MYOPIA HUNT CLUB NEAR BOSTON.

HUNTER'S SIZZLING 68

The first, and last, time the U.S. Open is held at Englewood Country Club in New Jersey, David Hunter scorches the layout in 1909 with a first-round 68. Hunter's round marks the first sub-70 score in Open history but he can't keep up the pace. He plummets with a second-round 84. Eventual champion George Sargent continues the assault, posting an event-best 290 total.

BROOKLINE BREAKTHROUGH

Francis Ouimet was a fixture at The Brookline Country Club. The 20 year old grew up across the street and learned the game as a caddie on the course, but not even the club's membership thought much of his chances when the 1913 U.S. Open was staged at the Boston-area course. Ouimet's rounds of 77–74–74–79 were good enough to force a playoff against legends Harry Vardon and Ted Ray, and the young man crafted a steady 72 in extra holes to take the title. Ouimet became the first amateur to win the U.S. Open and, more importantly, his working-man demeanor helped spark interest in the game throughout the United States.

AGELESS VARDON WINS SIXTH

Timing and a timeless swing allowed Harry Vardon to win his sixth British Open title in 1914, securing his place atop the list of British champions. Despite an unexplained illness that nearly forced him to withdraw from the final round, Vardon, 44, finished three shots clear of J. H. Taylor. The next five British Opens were canceled because of the onset of World War I, denying the other two members of the Great Triumvirate (J. H. Taylor and James Braid) a chance to match Vardon's accomplishment.

FOOD CRITIC

NOT EVEN A BAD LOBSTER DINNER COULD STOP WALTER HAGEN AT THE 1914 U.S. OPEN. DESPITE BEING STRICKEN WITH FOOD POISONING, HAGEN BECAME THE FIRST PLAYER TO LEAD WIRE-TO-WIRE AND WIN THE OPEN.

QUIET LINKS

Following the example set by the British Open, the 1917 and '18 U.S. Opens and PGA Championships are canceled because of World War I. The U.S. Golf Association, however, did hold an event called the Open Patriotic Tournament. Proceeds from the event, which was won by Jock Hutchison, were donated to the Red Cross.

THIRD DAY'S A CHARM

In 1919, the U.S. Open is played over three days for the first time. Eighteen holes are scheduled for Days 1 and 2 followed by the closing 36 holes on the third day. A fifth playoff round is needed when Walter Hagen and Michael J. Brady finish 72 holes tied at 301. Hagen wins by a stroke in extra holes.

THIRTEEN LUCKY FOR DUNCAN

In the first British Open following World War I, George Duncan pulls off one of the greatest comebacks in major championship history in 1920. Thirteen shots behind leader Abe Mitchell after 36 holes, Duncan charges back to win the event by two strokes.

LONG JIM GETS PRESIDENTIAL TREATMENT

Following his nine-stroke victory at the 1921 U.S. Open, Long Jim Barnes, whose nickname was a byproduct of his prodigious drives, was awarded the Open trophy by U.S. President Warren G. Harding.

FREE RIDE ENDS

For the first time, the U.S. Golf Association charges admission into the 1922 U.S. Open at Skokie Country Club near Chicago. For the sum of $1, fans are treated to Gene Sarazen's first major victory.

DROUGHT ENDS FOR JONES

BOBBY JONES FINALLY GETS OFF THE SCHNEIDE, WINNING HIS FIRST MAJOR CHAMPIONSHIP AT THE 1923 U.S. OPEN. JONES ENDS "SEVEN LEAN YEARS" WITHOUT A TITLE DESPITE A DOUBLE-BOGEY ON THE 72ND HOLE. HE MAKES UP FOR THE GAFFE IN EXTRA HOLES, BEATING BOBBY CRUICKSHANK, 76–78.

IN A RUT

Leo Diegel begins the afternoon round of his 36-hole final match at the 1926 PGA Championship just 2-down to Walter Hagen. From there things just get worse. On the first hole in the afternoon, Diegel's approach flies over the green and rolls under a car. When the car is moved, Diegel's golf ball nestles into a deep rut and it takes him three swings to get it on the green. He loses the hole and eventually the match, 5 and 3.

ARMOUR ARRIVES

Tommy Armour, who was severely wounded while serving in the British military during World War I, emerges as a major championship contender at the 1927 U.S. Open. Armour birdies the 72nd hole to tie Harry Cooper and wins the title in a playoff.

IMPREGNABLE QUADRILATERAL

Many in the press had flirted with the idea of Bobby Jones winning all four of the era's major championships. *New York Sun* reporter George Trevor even dubbed the achievement "the Impregnable quadrilateral." One player, Bobby Cruickshank, even wagered on Jones reaching golf's grand pinnacle. But after a sub-par year in 1929, during which Jones lost in the first round of match play at the U.S. Amateur, few could have considered 1930 the year of the Grand Slam. Jones's year, however, turned into the game's most hallowed achievement.

• May's British Amateur proves to be Jones's greatest hurdle. It's the only major he hasn't won and the closest he comes to defeat. In the fourth round, defending champion Cyril Tolley narrowly misses a 12-foot birdie putt on the final hole that would have ended Jones's run before it began. Jones rallies to win the match on the first extra hole and he easily defeats Roger Wethered in the final to take the title.

• Jones edges the field at the British Open at Hoylake in June, beating Macdonald Smith and Leo Diegel by two strokes and breaking the course record by 10 shots with his 291 total.

• With birdies at three of his last six holes, Jones wins the U.S. Open at Interlachen Country Club in Minnesota to set up a pressure-packed final run at the Slam.

• At the site of his first USGA championship, Merion Cricket Club, Jones completes the Grand Slam with a convincing 8-and-7 finals victory over Eugene V. Homans at the U.S. Amateur.

"LAWRENCE OF THE LINKS"

Although not as well known as Bobby Jones or as ostentatious as Walter Hagen, Tommy Armour had a style all his own. Dubbed the "Lawrence (as in Arabia) of the Links" by one journalist, Armour became the first professional to have won four major titles with his victory at the 1931 British Open at Carnoustie Golf Club. Armour added the Claret Jug to his trophies from the 1927 U.S. and Canadian Opens and 1930 PGA Championship.

PUNCHLESS PGA

In a PGA Championship lacking in star power, Olin Dutra was almost untouchable at Minnesota's Keller Golf Club in 1932. Dutra played his 196 holes in 19 under par and easily took the title, beating Frank Walsh in the final, 4 and 3. Among those who didn't qualify for the event were Tommy Armour, Harry Cooper, and Gene Sarazen, who won the 1932 U.S. and British Opens and was voted the Associated Press Athlete of the Year.

AMATEUR HOUR

Johnny Goodman builds a six-stroke lead through three rounds at the 1933 U.S. Open and holds on to take the title when Ralph Guldahl bogeys the 72nd hole. Goodman, who until his Open victory was best known for his upset victory over Bobby Jones in the first round of the 1929 U.S. Amateur, becomes the fifth and final amateur to win the U.S. Open.

AN AZALEA BY ANY OTHER NAME

Originally dubbed the Augusta National Invitation Tournament, club co-founder Cliff Roberts proposes calling the event the Masters, but Bobby Jones balks, thinking the name to be too presumptuous. Horton Smith wins the first event in 1934, and Jones agrees to change the name to the Masters.

CRUICKSHANK TAKES MAJOR BLOW

In the hunt with nine holes remaining at the 1934 U.S. Open, Bobby Cruickshank is so relieved when his approach shot into the 64th hole bounces off a rock and onto the green he tosses his club in the air to celebrate. The club hits Cruickshank on the head, knocking him unconscious. Cruickshank recovers but struggles to a closing 76 to finish two shots behind Olin Dutra.

"SHOT HEARD 'ROUND THE WORLD"

Gene Sarazen's 4-wood second shot into Augusta National's 15th green was a defining moment for the Masters, if not for Sarazen himself. Yet what is often forgotten is what followed Sarazen's "Shot heard 'round the world" and tournament-tying double eagle-2 on the par-5 hole. Sarazen parred the final three holes and breezed past a shell-shocked Craig Wood in a 36-hole playoff to win the 1935 Masters.

LONGSHOTS SHINE

Neither Sam Parks Jr. nor Alfred Perry were considered serious contenders for any titles in 1935, but both made their mark on the major stage. Parks was a member of Oakmont Country Club and used his local knowledge to win the U.S. Open, while Perry tied the tournament record with a 283 total to take the British Open.

SECOND FIDDLE

Moments after Horton Smith has completed his come-from-behind victory at the 1936 Masters, runner-up Harry Cooper turns to tournament-host Bobby Jones and says: "It seems that it was not intended for me to ever win a major tournament." His words prove to be prophetic a few months later when Cooper is edged by dark-horse Tony Manero at the U.S. Open.

MASTERFUL COMEBACK FOR NELSON

Lifted by a final-round eagle on Augusta National's par-5 13th, Byron Nelson soars from six strokes back to deny Ralph Guldahl and win his first major title at the 1937 Masters.

SLAMMIN' SAMMY

In just his third PGA Tour event, Sam Snead wins the Oakland (California) Open and arrives at Michigan's Oakland Hills Country Club for the 1937 U.S. Open filled with confidence. Snead leads by a shot through 54 holes but, despite a closing 71, is overtaken by a charging Ralph Guldahl, who posts an Open-record 281 total.

Runyan rolls

Outdriven and overshadowed by his high-profile opponent for most of the final match, Paul Runyan pulls off a classic match-play upset at the 1938 PGA Championship. Although he finds himself 40 yards behind fellow finalist Sam Snead on every drive, Runyan posts an 8-and-7 victory for his second PGA title.

GULDAHL'S MAJOR RUN

Ralph Guldahl's one-stroke victory at the 1939 Masters completes a rousing three-year roll that includes six major titles, three of which came at the Western Open, and a leadership role on the 1937 Ryder Cup team.

SARAZEN COMES UP SHORT

Eighteen years after winning his first U.S. Open, Gene Sarazen's bid to add another Open trophy to his mantel comes up three shots short. Sarazen, 38, loses to Lawson Little, 70–73, in a playoff at the 1940 championship.

BEN'S BEST NOT ENOUGH

Although 1940 was a breakthrough year for Ben Hogan, who won three Tour events and the circuit's money title, his season is marred when he fails to qualify for the U.S. Open at Canterbury Golf Club in Ohio.

SECOND NO MORE

After finishing second at the first two Masters, Craig Wood ends his major drought with a three-stroke victory in 1941 at Augusta National. A few weeks later, he wins the U.S. Open by the same margin despite a painful back injury that forces him to wear a corset for support. Because of the United States' entry into World War II, the 1941 Open is the last played until 1946.

WINNING THE WAR AT HOME

In 1944, with the war turning in the Allies favor, the PGA resumes play of the PGA Championship. It's the first major championship played in two years and is won by Bob Hamilton, who stuns 10-to-1 favorite Byron Nelson in the final match.

OUT OF THE MONEY

At the urging of his equipment sponsors, Sam Snead plays the 1946 British Open. In the first Open Championship since 1939, Snead laps the field by four strokes but claims the $600 winner's check doesn't cover the $1,000 it cost him to travel to St. Andrews for the event.

A CHAMPION BY ANY MEASURE

In the first U.S. Open to be televised locally, Lew Worsham nips Sam Snead by a stroke in an 18-hole playoff at the 1947 championship. On the final hole of the playoff, Snead misses a short putt after Worsham asks for a measurement.

HARMON MAKES A SPLASH

From a shallow creek that guards the front of the 13th green at Augusta National, Claude Harmon splashes a chip out and makes par on his way to his fourth sub-par round and a five-stroke victory at the 1948 Masters.

HENRY THE GREAT

At 41, Henry Cotton wins his third British Open. The 1948 victory marks the distinguished Englishman's first in the Open Championship since 1937.

HOUSE CALL

DR. CARY MIDDLECOFF, A FORMER DENTIST TURNED PROFESSIONAL, HOLDS OFF CLAYTON HEAFNER DURING A HEATED FINAL ROUND AT THE 1949 U.S. OPEN AT MEDINAH COUNTRY CLUB.

SUGGS UNSTOPPABLE

The newly formed LPGA hosts the 1949 U.S. Women's Open but the results are familiar. Louise Suggs blows away the field by a record 14 strokes.

AN OPEN MIRACLE

Just 16 months after a near-fatal car accident, Ben Hogan returns to the winner's circle to complete one of the game's most inspiring comebacks at the 1950 U.S. Open. Weary from his injuries, Hogan opens with rounds of 72–74 at Merion Golf Club and holds on over a grueling 36-hole final day to force a playoff. With his ailing legs wrapped in bandages, Hogan cruises to a 69 in the playoff to win his second Open title.

NO BEAUTY CONTEST

Chandler Harper is more magician than major champion at the 1950 PGA Championship, but he proves to be resilient enough to take the title. In what is considered one of the sloppiest PGA finals, Harper struggles to a 75 in the morning round but still leads 3 up. He's marginally better in the afternoon and closes out Henry Williams Jr., 4 and 3.

A ROARING START FOR RAWLS

ROOKIE BETSY RAWLS OPENS WITH ROUNDS OF 73–71 AT THE 1951 U.S. WOMEN'S OPEN AND NEVER LOOKS BACK AS SHE ROLLS TO A FIVE-STROKE VICTORY.

Julius joins stars

Julius Boros makes his first appearance on the major stage with a convincing breakthrough at the 1952 U.S. Open. His four-stroke victory comes less than a year after his wife died following childbirth.

BROTHERLY BREAKTHROUGH

After six major misses for the Turnesa clan, Jim Turnesa finally gets it right at the 1952 PGA Championship. Turnesa beats Chick Harbert, 1 up, in the finals to claim the Wanamaker Trophy. Prior to Jim's victory, the Turnesas— including brothers Joe and Mike—had finished runner-up at a major four times and third twice.

RAWLS ROLLS

In the first U.S. Women's Open sponsored by the USGA, Betsy Rawls gets the best of Jackie Pung in a playoff, 71–77. The 1953 championship is Rawls's second Open victory and will mark the second time Pung is denied the title.

The Hogan Slam

In his only British Open, Ben Hogan is untouchable on his way to a four-stroke rout at Carnoustie in 1953. Following commanding victories at the Masters and U.S. Open, Hogan skips the PGA Championship to spend two weeks learning the nuances of links golf at Carnoustie. The extra time pays off, but it also denies Hogan a shot at winning the single-season Grand Slam.

A DOUBLE TRIUMPH FOR BABE

Just over a year after undergoing surgery for colon cancer, Babe Didrikson Zaharias caps her comeback with an inspiring victory at the 1954 U.S. Women's Open. Didrikson builds a six-stroke, mid-way lead at hilly Salem Country Club in Massachusetts and, after an afternoon nap between her final two rounds, pulls away for a 12-shot romp.

PATTON'S POOR SWING

Billy Joe Patton's attempt to become the first amateur to win the Masters in 1954 is sunk when the carefree sentimental favorite hits his second shot into the creek fronting the 13th green. Patton makes double bogey and finishes two strokes back.

Must-see TV

His left arm crippled from a childhood accident, Ed Furgol scores an emotional victory over Gene Littler at the 1954 U.S. Open. The moving, one-stroke conquest is the first Open televised nationally.

FOREIGN INTEREST

Uruguay's Fay Crocker wins the 1955 U.S. Women's Open. Crocker, who won her country's amateur championship 20 times, is the first foreign-born player to win the championship.

MIDDLECOFF'S MASTERPIECE

Cary Middlecoff's 75-foot eagle putt at No. 13 during Round 2 of the 1955 Masters sends a shock wave through Augusta National's pine trees and his then-tournament record 65 sets a mark no one else can match. Middlecoff follows with rounds of 72–70 to win by seven shots.

AN UPSET FOR THE AGES

That Ben Hogan didn't win the 1955 U.S. Open was surprising enough. That he lost to a little-regarded teaching pro from an Iowa municipal course is one of the game's greatest upsets. Jack Fleck matched Hogan's 287 total with two late birdies in the final round and, thanks to a red-hot putter, he stunned the legend in an 18-hole playoff, 69–72.

MASTER'S MISS HARD ON VENTURI

Two years after Billy Joe Patton's brush with Masters fame, another amateur entered the final round at Augusta National with a chance to make history. Through 54 holes at the 1956 tournament, 24-year-old Ken Venturi was nearly flawless, building a four-stroke lead. But like Patton before him, Sunday at the Masters was too overwhelming for him and he limped home with a closing 80 to lose by one shot.

THOMSON'S TRIFECTA

PETER THOMSON WINS THE 1956 BRITISH OPEN AT HOYLAKE IN ENGLAND. IT'S THE AUSTRALIAN'S THIRD CONSECUTIVE BRITISH OPEN TITLE.

A CHAMPION UNDONE

Moments after signing for a final-round 72 and what appears to be a tournament-winning 298 total at the 1957 U.S. Women's Open, Jackie Pung is disqualified because of an incorrect scorecard. Pung inadvertently signs for a 5 on the fourth hole instead of the correct score of 6. The title and $1,800 winner's check is awarded to Betsy Rawls with a 299 total. Pung would never win a major title. Some solace for Pung, Winged Foot club members and journalists collect $2,500 to donate to the jilted champion.

FORD RACES TO VICTORY

Trailing by three strokes through 54 holes, Doug Ford caps his Sunday charge at the 1957 Masters with a birdie from the bunker at the 18th for a three-shot victory.

HEBERT CLOSES BOOK ON MATCH PLAY

Lionel Hebert downs Dow Finsterwald in the final of the 1957 PGA Championship, 2 and 1. The victory is Hebert's first on the PGA Tour and marks the last PGA decided by match play.

A KING IS BORN

Arnold Palmer's career would be defined by his slashing, hard-swinging style, and at the 1958 Masters "The King" gave the golf world its first glimpse of that greatness. Following a sloppy bogey at No. 10 on Sunday, Palmer rips a 3-wood second shot to 18 feet on the par-5 13th and coaxes the putt into the hole. The 28 year old from Western Pennsylvania would finish a shot ahead of Doug Ford and Fred Hawkins to claim the first of his four green jackets.

A BOLT OF LIGHTNING

FIERY TOMMY BOLT GOES WIRE-TO-WIRE TO WIN THE 1958 U.S. OPEN BY FOUR STROKES. IT IS BOLT'S ONLY MAJOR VICTORY.

MAJOR MILESTONE

At 40 years old, Patty Berg wins the 1958 Women's Western Open to claim the last of her 15 major titles. Berg won seven Westerns, seven Titleholder Championships, and a U.S. Women's Open.

A DAY OF REST

Saturday thunderstorms at the 1959 U.S. Open wash out Winged Foot Golf Club in New York and force the USGA to play the final round on Sunday for the first time. Billy Casper finishes a shot ahead of Bob Rosburg to take the title.

BLACK KNIGHTED

Gary Player, who would soon earn the nickname "Black Knight," edges Fred Bullock and Flory Van Donck by two shots at Muirfield in Scotland to win the 1959 British Open. It's Player's first major title.

"THE CHARGE"

In what would become known in golf lore as "The Charge," Arnold Palmer birdies his last two holes to win the 1960 Masters. Two months later, Arnie was at it again, driving the first green at Cherry Hills Country Club during the final round of the U.S. Open for a closing 65 and a two-stroke victory over amateur Jack Nicklaus. Palmer finishes the season with eight victories.

Century celebration

Kel Nagle wins the 1960 British Open at St. Andrews. It's the 100th playing of the Open Championship and the Australian is awarded the traditional Claret Jug as well as a slightly smaller version of the trophy to mark the occasion.

"MICKEY'S OPEN"

Mickey Wright plays just 17 events in 1961 and she wins 10 of those. The most impressive of her conquests is the U.S. Women's Open, which she wins in such a convincing fashion players dub the championship "Mickey's Open." Wright laps the field at Baltusrol Golf Club in New Jersey by six shots to claim her third Open title in four years.

A GRAND OPEN-ING FOR JACK

Newly minted professional Jack Nicklaus, 22, lays the foundation for one of the game's greatest rivalries when he ties Arnold Palmer after 72 holes at the 1962 U.S. Open and edges the older legend in an 18-hole playoff (71–74). A fact to figure in Nicklaus's victory: he three-putted just once in 90 holes. Said Palmer: "Now that the big guy's out of the cage, everybody better run for cover."

LINDSTROM WEATHERS STORM

In a driving rain, Murle Lindstrom rallies to win the 1962 U.S. Women's Open at the Dunes Golf and Beach Club in Myrtle Beach, South Carolina. It's Lindstrom's first victory on the LPGA and her 301 total is the last time the Women's Open is won with a score over the 300 mark.

OUT OF THE WOODS

With swirling, unpredictable winds that gust up to 35 mph for much of the event, Julius Boros survives a mid-round miscue at the 1963 U.S. Open to win his second national crown. After hitting into the trees on No. 13 during an 18-hole playoff and taking double bogey, Boros recovers to shoot 70 and edge Jacky Cupit and Arnold Palmer at The Country Club in Massachusetts.

NO SLUMP FOR SOPHOMORE NICKLAUS

IN HIS SECOND SEASON ON THE PGA TOUR IN 1963, JACK NICKLAUS FINISHES IN THE TOP 10 IN 17 OF HIS 24 EVENTS AND ADDS THE SECOND AND THIRD LEGS OF THE CAREER GRAND SLAM TO HIS RÉSUMÉ (MASTERS AND PGA CHAMPIONSHIP).

SOUTHPAW SPECIAL

Bob Charles beats Phil Rodgers in a 36-hole playoff to win the 1963 British Open, and becomes the first left-handed player to win a major championship.

BEATING THE HEAT

After having been sidelined by a pinched nerve in 1962, Ken Venturi overcomes searing temperatures and 36 grueling holes to win the 1964 U.S. Open at Congressional near Washington, D.C. It's the last year the USGA would play the final two rounds in a single day.

CHAMPAGNE TONY

Tony Lema—whose nickname "Champagne" was a salute to his quick wit and good-natured disposition—arrives at St. Andrews, Scotland, for the 1964 British Open just 36 hours before his first-round tee time. When his manager tries to explain the peculiar ways of the Old Course to him, Lema interrupts: "Just let me tee it up. I don't build courses, I play 'em." No one plays the Old Course better than Lema, who finishes with a 279 total for a five-stroke victory.

A REAL PLAYER

GARY PLAYER MATCHES KEL NAGLE SHOT-FOR-SHOT IN AN 18-HOLE PLAYOFF TO WIN THE 1965 U.S. OPEN AND BECOME THE THIRD PLAYER TO WIN ALL FOUR MODERN MAJOR CHAMPIONSHIPS. AT 29, THE SOUTH AFRICAN IS THE YOUNGEST TO RECORD THE CAREER GRAND SLAM.

JERSEY GIRL

Carol Mann fills the void left when defending champion Mickey Wright withdraws with a thumb injury. Mann finishes at 290 to win the 1965 U.S. Women's Open at Atlantic City Country Club in New Jersey. Although she would wrap up her LPGA career with 38 victories, the 1965 Open was her only major.

The King's crash

With nine holes to play in the 1966 U.S. Open, Arnold Palmer is in charge with a seven-stroke lead. That's when he becomes fixated on breaking Ben Hogan's 276 tournament-total record. Five sloppy bogeys later, Palmer finishes tied with Billy Casper. Casper wins the playoff by four shots. It was the worst collapse of Arnie's career.

THE GOLDEN SLAM

In 1966, Jack Nicklaus becomes the first player to win back-to-back Masters. Four months later, "The Golden Bear" nips Doug Sanders and Dave Thomas by a shot to win the British Open at Muirfield in Scotland and becomes the fourth player to win the career Grand Slam.

THE HAWK'S SWAN SONG

GRANTED A SPECIAL EXEMPTION BY THE USGA, BEN HOGAN PLAYS HIS FINAL U.S. OPEN IN 1967. AT 54, HOGAN FINISHES 34TH, 17 STROKES BEHIND WINNER JACK NICKLAUS.

TITLEHOLDERS' TIME COMES

A women's major since its debut in 1937, the Titleholders Championship is canceled in 1967 because of financial troubles. The event is revived for one year in 1972.

THE "MERRY MEX"

Lee Trevino, who will be nicknamed the "Merry Mex," becomes the first player to post four sub-70 rounds on his way to victory at the 1968 U.S. Open. The title is Trevino's first on the PGA Tour.

Milestone major

Julius Boros sneaks past Arnold Palmer by one stroke to win the 1968 PGA Championship. At 48 years old, Boros becomes the oldest major champion, and Palmer's $12,500 check for second place makes him the first player to reach $1 million in career earnings.

WEDDING WOWS

Seven weeks after getting married, Susie Maxwell Berning wins the 1968 U.S. Women's Open. Perennial contender Mickey Wright finishes three back.

AN ARMY OF ONE

Following a 14-year hitch in the U.S. Army, Orville Moody adds his name to the list of unlikely U.S. Open winners at the 1969 championship. With a crowded leaderboard closing in, Moody seals the victory with four consecutive pars to finish a shot ahead of Deane Beman, Al Geiberger, and Bob Rosburg.

JACKLIN ENDS BRITISH SLUMP

Tony Jacklin wins the 1969 British Open to become the first Englishman in 18 years to claim the Claret Jug.

A PLAYER PROTEST

Civil rights protesters disrupt play during the third round of the 1969 PGA Championship. The protesters target South African Gary Player, who finishes a shot behind winner Raymond Floyd.

CASPER SLAYS AUGUSTA GHOSTS

After a disappointing runner-up finish at the 1969 Masters, Billy Casper survives a difficult final round in 1970 to force a playoff with Gene Littler. In extra holes, Casper's putter powers him to victory, 69–74, and his first green jacket.

ST. ANDREWS SPECIAL

Doug Sanders misses a 3-foot par putt on the 72nd hole of the 1970 British Open to finish tied with Jack Nicklaus. In the playoff, Nicklaus drives the 18th green and edges Sanders, 72–73.

A GRAND DOUBLE

JACK NICKLAUS GOES WIRE-TO-WIRE TO WIN THE 1971 PGA CHAMPIONSHIP AND BECOME THE FIRST PLAYER TO WIN EVERY MAJOR CHAMPIONSHIP TWICE.

The last laugh

Always relaxed and rarely overcome by the moment, Lee Trevino begins his 18-hole playoff against Jack Nicklaus at the 1971 U.S. Open with a joke. As Nicklaus steps to the first tee at Merion Golf Club, Trevino playfully tosses a rubber snake at him. Trevino easily wins the playoff, 68–71, and caps his season with victories at the Canadian and British Opens.

IN SEARCH OF THE SLAM

In 1972, Jack Nicklaus wins the Masters and U.S. Open by three shots and arrives at the British Open with a chance of becoming the first player to win the modern Grand Slam. However, Nicklaus needs a final-round 66 to get into contention and Lee Trevino closes the door when he chips in for par on the 71st hole to win his second consecutive Open Championship.

MILLER'S MAGIC

Six strokes back at the start of the final round in the 1973 U.S. Open, Johnny Miller was nearly flawless on his way to a nine-birdie, one-bogey 63. The lowest round in Open history lifts Miller, who began his final 18 holes an hour before the third-round leaders, to a one-stroke victory at Oakmont Country Club.

AN OPEN PLAYER

The term "horses for courses" refers to certain players who excel on particular golf courses. In 1974, Hale Irwin began his love affair with U.S. Open venues. At the 1974 Open, Irwin finished at 7 over par and recorded 18 bogeys for the week, yet was two shots ahead of his nearest pursuer. Irwin's grinding, workman-like style proved to be a perfect fit for normally demanding U.S. Open venues.

TWO-FOR-TWO

Just two LPGA majors are played in 1974 and Sandra Haynie wins both of them. Haynie downs JoAnne Carner by two shots at the LPGA Championship, and she clips Carol Mann and Beth Stone by one at the U.S. Women's Open.

Masters' moment

While Gene Sarazen's double-eagle at the 1935 Masters sped the event's transition from quaint invitational to major championship, Jack Nicklaus's hard-fought victory in 1975 at Augusta National solidifies the tournament as the grandest of them all.

CRAMPTON HEATS UP FIRESTONE

Bruce Crampton shoots a tournament-record 63 in Round 2 of the 1975 PGA Championship at Firestone Country Club in Ohio, but he cools with a third-round 75 and finishes two shots behind winner Jack Nicklaus.

PALMER, SANDRA NOT ARNIE, WINS TWICE

In 1975, Sandra Palmer wins the LPGA's richest event, Colgate-Dinah Shore Winners Circle, and most prestigious, the U.S. Women's Open, on her way to becoming the Tour's player of the year.

FLOYD FINDS HIS WAY

After an impressive start, Raymond Floyd's career hits a dry spell when he fails to win an event from 1970–74. In fact, when he steps to the first tee of the 1976 Masters his name isn't even on the leaderboard. Rounds of 65–66–70–70 lift Floyd to the top of that board and to his only Masters title.

UNFORGETTABLE FINALÉ

The 1976 U.S. Open comes down to a single hole for four men. John Mahaffey, Tom Weiskopf, Al Geiberger, and Jerry Pate arrive at the last hole—a 460-yard, par-4 at Atlanta Athletic Club—all with a chance to win the event. Weiskopf and Geiberger hit poor drives and are forced to lay up with their second shots and Mahaffey hits into a water hazard. Pate, a flamboyant 22-year-old rookie, drives into the fairway and ropes a 5-iron to 2 feet for birdie and the title.

WHAT'S IN A NAME?

A NEW LPGA EVENT CALLED THE LADIES' MASTERS DRAWS THE IRE OF AUGUSTA NATIONAL. THE CLUB FORCES LPGA OFFICIALS TO CHANGE THE EVENT'S NAME, BUT IN NOVEMBER 1976 A FEDERAL JUDGE RULES THE TOURNAMENT CAN BE CALLED THE LADIES' MASTERS.

UNSHAKABLE GREEN

A death threat on the eve of the final round of the 1977 U.S. Open did little to rattle Hubert Green. With a police escort, Green fired a final-round 70 to win by one shot.

Sudden solution

Lanny Wadkins and Gene Littler finish 72 holes tied at the 1977 PGA Championship, forcing the first sudden-death playoff in major history. Wadkins holes his 6-foot par putt on the third extra hole to end a four-year victory slump.

NEVER DOWN, NEVER OUT

Trailing by seven strokes after 54 holes, Gary Player puts on a back-nine show during the final round of the 1978 Masters. The South African comes home in 30 strokes to become the event's oldest champion at 42.

DUE NORTH

Andy North avoids what could have been a timeless gaffe at the 1978 U.S. Open. Needing only a bogey to win, North hits his tee shot in thick rough, his approach into more rough, and his third shot into a greenside bunker. Fortunately, he chips to 4 feet and converts the putt to win by one shot.

SNEED UNRAVELS

Ed Sneed, who led by five strokes after the third round, bogeys his final three holes to finish in a tie with Tom Watson and Fuzzy Zoeller at the 1979 Masters. Zoeller wins the sudden-death playoff, the first in Masters history, with a birdie at the second extra hole.

Savvy Seve

At 22, Seve Ballesteros wins the 1979 British Open. The scrambling Spaniard saves his title chances on the 70th hole. After hitting into a nearby carpark, Ballesteros slashes his next shot onto the green and makes birdie.

THE HINKLE TREE

During Round 1 at the 1979 U.S. Open, journeyman pro Lon Hinkle plays his tee shot on Inverness Club's eighth hole down the adjacent 17th fairway, dramatically cutting the distance to the eighth green. Hinkle hits his second shot on the green and makes an easy two-putt birdie. That night, in an attempt to discourage Hinkle or anybody else from taking the shortcut again, the USGA plants a 20-foot-tall Black Hill spruce. "In a row of 60- or 70-year-old trees, it looked pretty puny. But it's all mine," Hinkle said.

Alcott ices Open

With temperatures approaching 100 degrees all week at Richland Country Club in Tennessee, Amy Alcott cruises to the 1980 U.S. Women's Open title. Alcott's 280 total breaks the event record by four shots and she finishes nine shots ahead of runner-up Hollis Stacy.

REDEMPTION FOR ROBERTO

Roberto De Vicenzo—best known for his scorecard mistake at the 1968 Masters—wins the first U.S. Senior Open in 1980.

HOME COOKING

LARRY NELSON—WHO LIVES LESS THAN 30 MINUTES FROM ATLANTA ATHLETIC CLUB, SITE OF THE 1981 PGA CHAMPIONSHIP—IS NEVER CHALLENGED ON HIS WAY TO A FOUR-STROKE VICTORY.

RECORD REQUIREMENT

Pat Bradley tops the U.S. Women's Open scoring record at the 1981 championship, finishing with a 279 total after weekend rounds of 68–66. Beth Daniel is second, just one shot back.

STADLER'S SECOND CHANCE

Craig Stadler stumbles to a closing-nine 40 on Sunday at the 1982 Masters to blow a five-shot lead, but he gets a second chance in the playoff when Dan

Pohl bogeys the first extra hole. The victory is the only major of Stadler's career.

THE CHIP

At the 1982 U.S. Open, with his ball buried deep in the Pebble Beach rough and 18 slick feet separating him from the flag on the scenic 17th hole, Tom Watson informs long-time caddie, Bruce Edwards, that he's going to chip the ball in. Moments later, Watson's unlikely birdie drops into the hole to secure the title and a place in golf history.

NELSON STORMS OAKMONT

The weather-plagued 1983 U.S. Open at Oakmont Country Club in Pennsylvania spills over into a Monday finish but the delays do little to unnerve Larry Nelson, who plays his final 36 holes in 10 under to edge third-round co-leader Tom Watson by a shot. During Round 2, two spectators are struck by lightning.

ROYAL RUN

All five of Tom Watson's British Open victories came at different courses, the last coming in 1983 at Royal Birkdale in England. Only Harry Vardon won more Open titles (six).

FUZZY ENDING

Greg Norman's 45-foot par putt on the 72nd hole of the 1984 U.S. Open gives him a share of the lead with Fuzzy Zoeller and seems to turn the event in the Australian's favor. But the easygoing Zoeller is fearless in an 18-hole playoff and laps Norman, 67–75. The 1984 Open is the first championship in 31 years that Arnold Palmer fails to qualify for.

ALABAMA SLAMMER

Using a putter he'd recently bought in Holland, Lee Trevino scorches Shoal Creek with four rounds in the 60s at the 1984 PGA Championship. Gary Player and Lanny Wadkins challenge briefly, but Trevino pulls away for a four-stroke victory.

STRANGE DAYS

Curtis Strange follows his opening 80 with a 65 in Round 2, to move onto the leaderboard at the 1985 Masters. Strange falls back on Sunday when he hits into the water on Nos. 13 and 15, opening the door for Bernhard Langer to take the green jacket.

NO SLOWING LOPEZ

DESPITE A TWO-STROKE PENALTY FOR SLOW PLAY IN THE FIRST ROUND OF THE 1985 LPGA CHAMPIONSHIP, NANCY LOPEZ CRUISES TO AN EIGHT-STROKE VICTORY.

A GOLDEN AGE

At 46 years old, Jack Nicklaus makes one final charge at the 1986 Masters. The Golden Bear closes with a back-nine 30 to claim his 18th, and perhaps most memorable, major victory. Three months later, 43-year-old Raymond Floyd shoots a near-flawless 66 in the final round of the U.S. Open to become the championship's oldest winner.

AN OPEN SCARE

FANS AND COMPETITORS ARE EVACUATED FROM THE COURSE DURING A PRACTICE ROUND AT THE 1986 U.S. WOMEN'S OPEN, BECAUSE OF A TOXIC CLOUD FROM A TRAIN DERAILMENT NEAR THE NCR GOLF CLUB IN OHIO.

Shark slayers

In 1986, Bob Tway holes out from a greenside bunker for birdie on the 72nd hole of the PGA Championship to deny Greg Norman. Tway's heroics started a trend of heartbreak for Norman, who is nicknamed "the Shark." The next year, Larry Mize chips in for birdie on the second playoff hole at Augusta National to foil Norman's title hopes.

STEADY IN SCOTLAND

More times than not, it's the turtle, not the hare, who wins major championships. At the 1987 British Open at Muirfield in Scotland, Nick Faldo proves to be the steadiest of them all. He closes with 18 unspectacular pars to win the championship by one stroke over Paul Azinger, who bogeys his 71st and 72nd holes.

PGA reaches boiling point

The combination of a demanding PGA National layout and sweltering south Florida temperatures leads to the highest winning score (287) in PGA Championship history. The 1987 event is won by Larry Nelson in a playoff, and is the last played in Florida.

AN AMERICAN CLASSIC

Seventy-five years after the original "United States vs. Great Britain" showdown, American Curtis Strange holds off Englishman Nick Faldo at the 1988 U.S. Open. The victory is Strange's first in a major and stirs memories of the 1913 Open, also played at The Country Club in Massachusetts, when America's Francis Ouimet outdueled British legends Harry Vardon and Ted Ray.

SANDY SPECIALIST

From an uphill lie in a fairway bunker, Sandy Lyle hits his approach shot on the 72nd hole of the 1988 Masters to 10 feet, holes the birdie putt, and beats Mark Calcavecchia by a shot.

LONG ROAD BACK FOR LITTLE

Following abdominal and arthroscopic knee surgery in 1983, Sally Little ends a six-year title drought with her 1988 victory at the du Maurier Classic.

HISTORIC HEARTBREAKS

The 1989 major season is defined by its collapses, not champions. Scott Hoch misses an 18-inch par putt on the first playoff hole at the Masters and loses to Nick Faldo. Tom Kite three-putts the fifth hole on Sunday to blow a three-stroke advantage at the U.S. Open. Greg Norman, no stranger to major pain, hits a bunker shot out-of-bounds during extra holes at the British Open. And Mike Reid crashes at the PGA Championship with a bogey, double bogey, par finish.

FOUR OF A KIND

In Round 1 at the 1989 U.S. Open, four players record holes-in-one on the same hole. Doug Weaver, Jerry Pate, Nick Price, and Mark Wiebe ace the 159-yard sixth hole at Oak Hill Country Club in New York. The odds of four players acing the same hole in one round? According to the National Hole-in-One Association, 8.7 million-to-1.

SHAKING THE STATUS QUO

Prior to the 1990 PGA Championship at Shoal Creek Country Club in Alabama, the club's founder sparks a firestorm when he publicly announces the club doesn't allow African-American members. The controversy that follows forces the PGA of America, PGA Tour, and USGA to create policies that ban their events from courses with discriminatory membership programs. Instead of changing their policies, many clubs stop hosting tournaments, including Butler National in Chicago, Cypress Point in California, and Aronimink in Pennsylvania.

All Hale Irwin

Playing on a special exemption from the USGA, 45-year-old Hale Irwin becomes the oldest U.S. Open champion when he shoots a closing 67 to tie Mike Donald at the 1990 championship. Irwin needs 19 more holes, an 18-hole playoff, and one sudden-death playoff hole, to finally shake Donald.

SHEEHAN STUMBLES

Leading by nine shots mid-way through the 1990 U.S. Women's Open, Patty Sheehan tumbles down the leaderboard on the weekend. She plays her final 27 holes in 8 over par and finishes a shot behind Betsy King.

LONG-SHOT DALY HAS HIS DAY

On the eve of the 1991 PGA Championship, Nick Price withdraws from the field to be with his wife, who is about to deliver the couple's first child. His withdrawal opens a spot for ninth-alternate John Daly, who drives all night to Crooked Stick Country Club in Indiana and stuns the golf world with his three-stroke victory.

DIVING IN

Amy Alcott sails to an eight-stroke victory at the 1991 Nabisco Dinah Shore and proceeds to dive into the lake adjacent the 18th hole at Mission Hills Country Club in Rancho Mirage, California. The "Dinah Dive" is now part of major tradition.

TRIUMPH AND TRAGEDY AT HAZELTINE NATIONAL

Scott Simpson bogeys his final three holes in an 18-hole playoff to blow a two-shot lead at the 1991 U.S. Open and open the door for Payne Stewart to win his first Open title. The week ends on a somber note, however, when spectator William Fadell is killed by lightning during the first round at Hazeltine National Golf Club in Minnesota.

NO DAY AT THE BEACH

After three calm days, the 1992 U.S. Open at Pebble Beach Golf Links turns into a survival test in Round 4. With winds up to 40 mph on Sunday, only five players break or match par and 20 others fail to break 80. Unfazed by the conditions, Tom Kite shoots a steady 72 for his first major crown.

SECOND TO NONE

After three runner-up finishes in the U.S. Women's Open, Patty Sheehan ends her suffering at the 1992 championship. With birdies at her final two holes, Sheehan ties Juli Inkster at 280, and she ends her Open jinx the next day in an 18-hole playoff, 72–74.

ANOTHER SPANISH WIZARD

Much like his mentor, Seve Ballesteros, José María Olazábal doesn't impress many people with his ability to drive the ball, but the Spaniard has a deft short-game that not even Augusta National's slick greens can baffle. Olazábal wins the 1994 Masters thanks to 30 one-putts for the week. He also chips-in twice and is a sizzling 6-for-6 in sand saves for the week.

PRICE-LESS

LESS THAN A MONTH AFTER WINNING THE BRITISH OPEN, NICK PRICE DRUBS THE FIELD AT THE 1994 PGA CHAMPIONSHIP BY SIX STROKES. PRICE'S 269 TOTAL BEATS THE PREVIOUS PGA RECORD BY TWO SHOTS AND IS THE LOWEST EVER IN ANY U.S. MAJOR.

OPEN NOT-SO-EASY FOR ELS

ERNIE ELS PLAYS HIS FIRST TWO HOLES AT THE 1994 U.S. OPEN IN 4 OVER PAR, BUT RALLIES TO PLAY THE REST OF THE WAY 1 UNDER. ELS AND COLIN MONTGOMERIE FINISH AN 18-HOLE PLAYOFF STILL TIED AND THE "BIG EASY" NEEDS TWO MORE HOLES TO WIN HIS FIRST MAJOR.

A Masters to remember

Just days after the death of his mentor, Harvey Penick, Ben Crenshaw birdies two of his final three holes to win the 1995 Masters. He breaks down crying following his final putt on the 72nd hole.

ONE MAJOR DOWN, MANY MORE TO COME

A year after being named the LPGA rookie of the year, Annika Sörenstam begins her assault on the record books with a one-stroke victory at the 1995 U.S. Women's Open. It is the Swede's first pro victory in the United States.

ANOTHER MELTDOWN FOR NORMAN

Three days after tying the course record, Greg Norman suffers the worst collapse in Masters history at the 1996 tournament. Leading Nick Faldo by six strokes through three rounds, the "Shark" slumps to a closing 78 while Faldo cards a 67 to win by five strokes.

MASTER-FUL DEBUT

In his first Masters as a pro, Tiger Woods tours his first nine at Augusta National in a pedestrian 4 over par. What follows that lukewarm start in 1997 becomes part of Masters lore. Woods closes with rounds of 66–65–69 to become the tournament's youngest champion at 21 years old. His 270 total and 12-shot margin of victory are also records.

END OF THE RAINBOW

In an emotional final round at the 1997 PGA Championship, Davis Love III outlasts close friend Justin Leonard to win his first major. Under a rainbow that had formed over Winged Foot Golf Club's 18th green, Love dedicates the victory to his father, late club pro David Love Jr., who died in a plane crash in 1988.

LEAVING HIS MARK

Mark O'Meara birdies three of his final four holes to win the 1998 Masters and end a 0-for-56 slump in the majors. The 41 year old completes his ageless summer a few months later when he edges Brian Watts in a playoff to win the British Open.

Youth is served

Nineteen-year-old professional Se Ri Pak needs 20 extra holes to deny amateur Jenny Chuasiriporn and win the 1998 U.S. Women's Open. Pak and Chuasiriporn finish 72 holes tied at 272 and fire matching 73s in the playoff. At the second sudden-death hole, Pak holes an 18-footer for the title.

COLLAPSE AT CARNOUSTIE

With a three-stroke lead with one hole to play at the 1999 British Open, Jean Van de Velde swings his way to golf infamy. After a poor drive on the 18th hole at Carnoustie Golf Links in Scotland, the Frenchman ricochets his next shot off the grandstand and into thick rough. From the rough, he hits into the water of Barry Burn on his way to a triple-bogey, which forces a playoff. Paul Lawrie, who began the day 10 shots out of the lead, wins to become the first Scotsman to claim the Claret Jug on Scottish soil in 68 years. "Don't be sad. I made plenty of friends because a Scottish man won. So, at least that's something," Van de Velde said after his collapse.

TIGER WEATHERS EL NIÑO

Tiger Woods wins his second major at the 1999 PGA Championship, but the week belongs to fearless young Spaniard Sergio García. With a furious back-nine charge, García—whose nickname is El Niño—cuts the lead to one shot, but Woods closes with 72 to claim his first Wanamaker Trophy.

TIGER SLAM

A first-round 75 foils Tiger Woods's title hopes at the 2000 Masters, but he is virtually unstoppable the rest of the season. He wins the U.S. Open at Pebble Beach by 15 strokes and completes his year with victories at the PGA Championship and British Open, where at 24, he becomes the youngest player to complete the career Grand Slam. The following spring, Woods wins his second Masters to become the first player to hold all four modern major championships at one time—a feat dubbed "The Tiger Slam."

ADIEU TO DU MAURIER

Because of sponsorship issues, the du Maurier Classic—a women's major since 1979—is held for the final time in 2000. The Women's British Open, which was added to the LPGA schedule in 1994, ascends to major status in 2001.

WORLDLY WEBB

KARRIE WEBB WINS THE 2001 U.S. WOMEN'S OPEN BY EIGHT SHOTS. IT'S THE AUSTRALIAN'S SECOND CONSECUTIVE OPEN TRIUMPH AND SHE FOLLOWS WITH A VICTORY AT THE LPGA CHAMPIONSHIP.

RELIEF FOR RETIEF

Retief Goosen misses a 2-foot putt for par at the 72nd hole to slip into a tie with Mark Brooks at the 2001 U.S. Open. The South African redeems himself the next day in extra holes, one-putting eight of his first 10 holes on his way to an easy two-shot victory.

DAVID SLAYS GOLIATH

David Toms denies Phil Mickelson, one of the PGA Tour's top performers but winless in the majors, at the 2001 PGA Championship, thanks to a brave decision on the final hole. With a one-stroke lead, Toms hits his drive on the 72nd hole into the right rough. He considers hitting 5-wood to the small, well-protected green, but instead hits a wedge shot to 88 yards. From there, Toms hits another wedge shot to 12 feet and holes the par putt to claim the title. Afterward, when asked why he decided to lay up, Toms said: "I might still be playing that hole if I would have gone for the green."

PRAIRIE LIVING

Juli Inkster wins the 2002 U.S. Women's Open at Prairie Dunes Country Club in Kansas, which was also the site of her 1980 U.S. Women's Amateur triumph. Inkster is just the second player—along with Jack Nicklaus—to win an Open at the same site they won an Amateur.

FROM RAGS TO RICHES

Rich Beem ignites a spate of unknown major champions with his stunner at the 2002 PGA Championship. Beem—who'd given up golf seven years earlier to sell car stereos and cell phones— holds off top-ranked Tiger Woods to win his first major. The next year, Ben Curtis claims the British Open title just seven months after earning his card at PGA Tour Qualifying School and Shaun Micheel wins his first Tour title at the PGA.

A lefty gets it right

Mike Weir plays 18 bogey-free holes on Sunday to finish tied with Len Mattiace at the 2003 Masters, and becomes the first left-hander to claim the green jacket. Weir also becomes the first Canadian to win a men's major. A year later, fellow southpaw Phil Mickelson follows Weir to the winner's circle at the Masters to collect his first major title.

TWO STROKES FROM A SLAM

Two shots, two swings of the club, cost Annika Sörenstam a shot at the single-year Grand Slam in 2003. She began the year with a runner-up finish at the Kraft Nabisco Championship. Following her victory at the LPGA Championship, a 4-wood second shot to the 72nd green at the U.S. Women's Open led to a bogey. She finished fourth, but wrapped up her year by winning the Women's British Open.

SAYONARA SLAM

IN 2000, WHEN JACK NICKLAUS PLAYS IN HIS FINAL U.S.
OPEN AND PGA CHAMPIONSHIP, TIGER WOODS RUNS
AWAY WITH BOTH TITLES. IN 2005, WOODS AND NICKLAUS
COMPLETE THE FAREWELL SLAM, OF SORTS, WHEN THE
"GOLDEN BEAR" PLAYS HIS FINAL MASTERS AND BRITISH
OPEN. WOODS EASILY WINS BOTH. "I WISH HE'D KEEP
RETIRING," WOODS SAID.

GRACE UNDER PRESSURE

Grace Park birdies the final hole of the 2004 LPGA
Kraft Nabisco Championship to win her first major.
The future of the game is in close pursuit, however.
Seventeen-year-old wunderkind Aree Song finishes a
shot back, while 14-year-old Michelle Wie—who just
weeks earlier missed the cut in the PGA Tour's Sony
Open by one shot—posts a fourth-place showing.

BIRDIE MAKER

Annika Sörenstam begins 2005 with easy victories
at the Kraft Nabisco Championship and LPGA
Championship, but her Grand Slam bid is denied
a few weeks later at the U.S. Women's Open when
appropriately named Birdie Kim holes her bunker
shot at the 72nd hole for a birdie and the title.

Playing fields

"*The ardent golfer would play Mount Everest if somebody put a flagstick on top.*"

Pete Dye

THE HOME OF GOLF

Although golf on the Old Course in St. Andrews, Scotland, has been played in one form or another for 500 years, one of the earliest known references to the ancient links was in 1553 when the Archbishop of St. Andrews issued a decree giving the local populace the right to play golf on the course. In 1754, the St. Andrews Society of Golfers (later the Royal and Ancient Golf Club of St. Andrews) was formed, and 10 years later the layout converted from 22 to 18 holes.

SOUTHERN COMFORT

In 1786, the South Carolina Golf Club was founded in Charleston, South Carolina. The club—which was disbanded about 25 years later—is regarded by many historians as the first golf club in the United States.

A FORTRESS FOR THE AGES

The course at North Berwick Golf Club in Scotland dates back to 1832, making it the second oldest club, behind St. Andrews, to have continuous play. But the club's most lasting legacy is derived from its 15th hole, which is a shortish par 3 with a green that is wider than it is deep and angles diagonally away from the tee box. Upon his return from the Crimean War, British army officer John White-Melville called the 15th "Redan," after the formidable fortress he had encountered in southern Russia. Today, many of the world's greatest courses have versions of North Berwick's Redan hole.

PRESTWICK'S PLACE IN HISTORY

The first British Open was played at Prestwick Golf Club in Scotland in 1860. The original 12-hole layout was extended in 1883 to 18 holes by Old Tom Morris. In total, Prestwick has hosted 24 Open Championships.

OLD HANDS MOLD OLD COURSE

Although Mother Nature is credited for designing the Old Course at St. Andrews, Scotland, Old Tom Morris's handiwork is prevalent throughout the ancient links. In 1864, Morris was appointed "conservator" of the Old Course and a year later he built the 18th green. In 1870, Morris added what is now the first hole.

RACY PAST

Originally built on the horseracing track of the Liverpool Hunt Club, Royal Liverpool Golf Club in Hoylake, England, still clings to its dual past. The original saddling bell hangs in the clubhouse and many of the holes still honor that tradition with horseracing names like Course and Stand. Originally built in 1869, Royal Liverpool was redesigned and extended to 18 holes in 1871.

CANADIAN ROYALTY

Although members relocated from the original layout in 1959, the club at Royal Montreal is considered the oldest continuous golf club in North America. The original course was built in 1873, 15 years before the first club in the United States.

Field of shinty

Machrihanish Golf Club opens in 1876 and is immediately lauded as one of the best. Designed by Old Tom Morris, the course's name is derived from the Scottish term Machair-an-lomain, or "field of the shinty." Shinty was a golf precursor played with large clubs curved at one end, similar to the hockey sticks of today.

IRISH ROYALTY

ROYAL BELFAST IN NORTHERN IRELAND WAS THE FIRST CLUB GOLF COURSE IN IRELAND AND THE COUNTRY'S FIRST TO RECEIVE A "ROYAL" DESIGNATION.

THE BEST OF BIARRITZ

One of the most copied elements of golf course design is the Biarritz green. Created by Willie Dunn in Biarritz, France, in the late 1880s, a Biarritz green features a deep gully bisecting its middle. The gully, which is manicured the same as the rest of the green, usually runs from side-to-side. One of the most famous Biarritz greens is the fifth hole at Fishers Island Golf Club in New York, which features two bunkers on either side of the putting surface and a bay to the right.

Team effort

Alex Finley is listed as the original architect of Pittsburgh Field Club in 1882. But if Finley were alive today he probably wouldn't recognize the layout. A total of nine designers have had their influence on this course over the years, including the likes of A. W. Tillinghast and Donald Ross.

PORTRUSH PERFECTION

Royal Portrush Golf Club opens in 1888 under the name County Club, and nine years later hosts Ireland's first professional tournament. The club is renamed Royal Portrush in 1895 and in 1947 H. S. Colt redesigns the layout. Four years later, Portrush becomes the country's first course to host a British Open.

ON THE MOVE

The Honorable Company of Edinburgh Golfers abandons the deteriorating Leith Links in 1836 for a new layout in Musselburgh. The company moves again in 1891, from the crowded Musselburgh course to its permanent home in Muirfield, which is designed by Old Tom Morris. The new 18 holes at Muirfield are not embraced at first, earning the disparaging nickname "watter meddie." The Muirfield track is substantially redesigned throughout the years, most notably in 1928 when H. S. Colt creates a two-loop plan.

Old Course tribute

Charles Blair Macdonald designs Chicago Golf Club as an ode to the Old Course in St. Andrews, Scotland. Chicago GC, which was founded in 1892 and is widely credited as being the oldest 18-hole course in the United States, features an almost exact replica of the Old Course's 17th hole, without the railroad shack and blind tee shot.

SOMETHING NEW

Shortly after the completion of the rail line into St. Andrews, the Old Course is overrun with more players than it can accommodate. As a result, officials conclude the area needs another layout so they build the New Course. The name is a bit misleading in modern times, however. The New Course opened for play in 1895.

BALTUS ROLL

New Jersey's Baltusrol Golf Club opened as a nine-hole course in 1895 on land owned by a farmer named Baltus Roll, who was killed on the land years earlier. The course was expanded to 18 holes in 1901 and has hosted seven U.S. Opens as well as a PGA Championship.

CLEANING UP THE GARBAGE

ALTHOUGH TODAY RENOWNED AS A CLASSIC LAYOUT, POSH LOS ANGELES COUNTRY CLUB HAD SOMETHING OF A TRASHY BEGINNING. IN 1897, CLUB MEMBERS RENTED A 16-ACRE PARCEL OF LAND THAT WAS ONCE USED AS A GARBAGE DUMP.

NAIRN GETS ITS DAY

On 60 acres donated by Sir Alexander Dunbar, Nairn Golf Club in Scotland opens in 1899. Although too short and confined ever to host a British Open, Nairn is pulled into the Walker Cup rotation in 1999.

"CHURCH PEW" PUNISHMENT

Following months of anticipation, Henry and William Fownes complete Oakmont Country Club in 1903. Built on a hill north of Pittsburgh, the layout quickly earns a reputation as a demanding track with its fast, undulating greens and the "church pew" bunker that lays between the third and fourth fairways. The Fownes' philosophy was clear: "A shot poorly played should be a shot irrevocably lost."

MAKING A MASTERPIECE

The original course opened in 1903, but what Donald Ross left behind at venerable Pinehurst No. 2 in North Carolina is something much more refined. Ross lived in a house adjacent No. 2 for years, and constantly tweaked and perfected its turtle-backed greens and low-lying collection areas.

HISTORIC DEBUT

Merion Cricket Club, the Pennsylvania layout that is later renamed Merion Golf Club, hosts the 1904 U.S. Women's Amateur, which is won by Georgianna Bishop. It is the first of 16 U.S. Golf Association championships held at the venerable club.

NATIONAL TREASURE

Charles Blair Macdonald was a decent player—having won the 1895 U.S. Amateur—and an influential member of the U.S. Golf Association. But Macdonald's lasting legacy is the courses he designed, and one of the greatest layouts he created was the National Golf Links of America in Southampton, New York, which opened in 1911.

SHORT BUT STOUT

HUGH WILSON'S SHORT BUT CHALLENGING EAST COURSE AT MERION CRICKET CLUB IN PENNSYLVANIA OPENS IN 1912. THE LAYOUT IS LATER THE SITE OF BOBBY JONES'S GRAND-SLAM-CLINCHING VICTORY AT THE 1930 U.S. AMATEUR AND BEN HOGAN'S EMOTIONAL TRIUMPH AT THE 1950 U.S. OPEN.

SHAKE-UP AT SAN FRANCISCO

Understated yet celebrated, the A. W. Tillinghast-designed San Francisco Golf Club opens in 1914 and remains nearly unchanged throughout the years. The only difference? Caddies claim the earthquake of 1989 altered some of the breaks in San Francisco GC's greens.

WANNAMOISETT STILL A WONDER

Of all Donald Ross's gems, Wannamoisett Country Club stands out as one of the most cherished. The Rhode Island layout opened in 1916 and has changed little through the years, retaining its peculiar par of 69 and most of Ross's original slopes and contours. The Donald Ross Society regards Wannamoisett so highly it uses its third hole as its logo.

Crump's dream course unfinished

George Crump dies on January 24, 1918, leaving the 12th through 15th holes at Pine Valley Golf Club in New Jersey unfinished. A year later, legendary architect H. S. Colt completes the course, which matures into the nation's most renowned layout. During the 1985 Walker Cup at Pine Valley, one British journalist writes that taking a divot "was like defacing a masterpiece." And Charlie Green, the chain-smoking Great Britain & Ireland captain, admits he felt guilty flicking cigarette ash onto the fairways.

DRINK UP

The ban on alcohol in the United States that began in 1919 sparks a construction phenomenon called anti-Prohibition courses. Layouts—like Gateway Cities Country Club in North Portal, Saskatchewan, Canada —feature nine holes in the U.S. and nine holes in Canada, with a clubhouse in Canada that serves copious amounts of alcohol.

A SHORT START

Of all the quirky links in the British Open rotation, Royal Lytham & St. Annes in England may be the oddest of them all. Royal Lytham—which underwent a redesign by H. S. Colt in 1919—is the only course in the rota to start on a par 3, and the layout also features back-to-back par 5s, nos. 6–7. Tony Jacklin said it was "a terrible strain" to begin with such a short, diabolical test.

THE ART OF MACKENZIE

Alister MacKenzie—the creator of some of the game's greatest courses, including Cypress Point in California and Georgia's Augusta National—publishes Golf Architecture *in 1920. The book is still considered the definitive story of golf course design.*

NUMBERS GAME

For the male members of Canterbury Golf Club—a Herbert Strong design that opened in 1921—the layout plays to a par of 72. For female members, the demanding Ohio layout is extended to a par 75.

TOUGH ACT

The West Course at Winged Foot Golf Club in New York is generally regarded, even nearly a century after it was built, as a demanding test, which is exactly what the original members wanted. When hired by the members of the New York Athletic Club in the early 1920s, A. W. Tillinghast was told to build a "man-size" golf course. Said Mark Brooks after winning the 1997 PGA Championship at Winged Foot: "There are about six hard holes out here, six very hard holes and six impossible holes."

AN OLYMPIC MOMENT

Built in 1924 by Willie Watson, The Olympic Club in San Francisco, California, features no water hazards and just a single fairway bunker. Yet during the 1998 U.S. Open the layout proved its real challenge lay on its slippery greens. During Round 2, Payne Stewart three-putted from 8 feet at No. 18 and lost the championship by a stroke. Tom Lehman four-putted the hole. "I crossed the line. It was a terrible mistake on my part," said U.S. Golf Association rules official Tom Meeks, who set the pin position at No. 18.

TILLIE TURNS OVER NEW LEAF

History will remember A. W. Tillinghast as one of the greatest golf course designers of the Golden Age of Golf Course Architecture (1910–1920). But before "Tillie" ever broke ground on his famous layouts at Winged Foot in New York or Baltusrol in New Jersey, he was a member of Philadelphia's scandalous "Kelly Street Gang."

What's in a name?

Chatham Country Club opens in 1926 in Massachusetts, but the membership quickly renames the layout Eastward Ho! Golf Club as a tribute to architect Herbert Fowler, who had designed the revered Westward Ho! Golf Club in England.

SOMETHING TO THINK ABOUT

Nearly every great golf course has a short par 4, a thinking man's hole that rewards brains over brawn. One of the most famous, and most copied, short par 4s is the 10th hole at Riviera Country Club in California. Built in 1926, Riviera's 10th is only 311 yards and tempts players to try and drive the green. But deep bunkers guard almost the entire putting surface, demanding a player's best shot if he/she wishes to risk it.

Down Under thunder

In 1926, at the urging of the Royal and Ancient Golf Club of St. Andrews, the members of Royal Melbourne Golf Club in Australia commission Alister MacKenzie to design the club's new West course. The club pays MacKenzie £1,000, considered an exorbitant price at the time, but much of the construction was left to Alex Russell after MacKenzie left Australia. Russell, using much of MacKenzie's design philosophies, also constructs the club's East course.

A TERROR IN THE CANADIAN ROCKIES

Dubbed "The Toronto Terror," Stanley Thompson is a larger-than-life character whose designs are equally unforgettable. Thompson's work on Banff Springs Golf Course, which opens in 1928 and sits high in the Canadian Rockies, is widely considered his greatest design. Thompson needs six years using horses, mules, railcars, and hundreds of men to create Banff Springs, rumored to be the first course to cost over $1 million to build.

GOLF ON HIGH

Atop its building in Philadelphia, the Penn Athletic Club opens an 18-hole miniature golf course in 1928.

MACKENZIE'S MONTEREY MASTERPIECE

Etched along the craggy California coast, Alister MacKenzie's Cypress Point Club opens in 1928. Among the celebrated collection of holes is the par-3 16th, which stretches 233 yards across the rolling Pacific Ocean. Said MacKenzie of the exclusive enclave: "I do not expect anyone will ever have the opportunity of constructing another course like Cypress Point, as I do not suppose anywhere in the world there is such a glorious combination of rocky coast, sand dunes, pine woods, and cypress trees."

New-look Pebble

Designed by Jack Neville and Douglas Grant in 1919, famed Pebble Beach Golf Links undergoes a redesign by H. Chandler Egan in 1928 that includes a complete overhaul of the 16th and 18th greens.

A HOME FOR HOGAN

Donald Ross considers it one of his best and Ben Hogan calls it home. Seminole Country Club opens in 1929 and almost immediately becomes a design classic.

MERION MOMENT

Prior to the 1930 U.S. Amateur at Merion Cricket Club, the course installs a state-of-the-art watering system. The investment is rewarded when Bobby Jones secures the final leg of the Grand Slam at Merion and attracts record crowds.

EARTHMOVER

DURING THE CONSTRUCTION OF NEW YORK'S BAYSIDE LINKS IN 1931, ALISTER MACKENZIE BECOMES THE FIRST ARCHITECT TO USE MODERN CONSTRUCTION EQUIPMENT TO MOLD A GOLF COURSE.

AUGUSTA IN BLOOM

The colorful azaleas and magnolias that dot the landscape at Augusta National Golf Club are as much a part of the annual Masters Tournament as the green jacket awarded to each year's champion. The flowers, however, were part of Augusta long before the venerable golf course opened in 1933. Augusta National is built on the site of a former plant nursery, which left behind hundreds of flora and fauna.

OF CAPTAINS AND CROWNS

Walton Heath in Surrey, England, holds the distinction of being the only club in the world to have had a reigning monarch as its captain. From 1935–1936, the then Prince of Wales became Edward VII while serving as the club's captain.

MINIMALIST MAXWELL

Unlike modern architects, who have taken earth moving and land shaping to new art forms, Perry Maxwell was a diehard minimalist. "The golf course should be there, not brought there," he said. While building Prairie Dunes Country Club in Hutchinson, Kansas, in 1935, Maxwell spent weeks walking the original 480-acre site before coming up with a layout.

WAR EFFORT

During World War II, many courses in Great Britain are plowed over or covered with debris to stop German warplanes from landing on them. Despite the obstacles, play continues in the Isles. Courses in the London area adopt wartime rules that include: "Competitors during gunfire or while bombs are falling may take cover without penalty."

AUGUSTA NATIONAL JOINS THE HERD

Like most courses at the time, Augusta National closes in 1943 and remains closed for the duration of World War II. During that time, officials open the pristine fairways to cattle for grazing.

HOME FIELD ADVANTAGE

Ohio State wins the 1945 NCAA Championship on the schooled-owned Scarlet Course. The Buckeyes are the first team to claim the national title on their own layout.

TURNBERRY'S AILSA IS ROCK SOLID

Built on property owned by a railway company that doubled as a wartime airfield, Turnberry Golf Club's Ailsa Course opens in 1946 and quickly gains a reputation as one of Scotland's most scenic layouts. The Ailsa Course—named for Ailsa Craig, a huge island made of volcanic rock about 10 miles off the Ayrshire coast—was the site of the historic "Duel in the Sun" between Tom Watson and Jack Nicklaus at the 1977 British Open.

HOGAN'S ALLEY

In less than 24 months, Ben Hogan turns Riviera Country Club into his personal playground and earns the elegant layout its nickname—Hogan's Alley. Hogan won the 1947 and '48 Los Angeles Opens at Riviera and made it a perfect sweep with his victory at the 1948 U.S. Open on the George C. Thomas-designed course.

Bing's best

The popular Bing Crosby Pro-Am moves from California's Rancho Santa Fe Country Club to the Monterey Peninsula in 1947. The original three-course rotation includes Pebble Beach Golf Links, Monterey Peninsula Country Club, and Cypress Point Country Club. Monterey Peninsula and Cypress Point are later removed from the rota and replaced with Spyglass Hill and Poppy Hills golf clubs.

THE GRAND STRAND

The first resort course to open after World War II was also the spark that ignited a South Carolina golf boom. The Robert Trent Jones Sr.-designed Dunes Golf and Beach Club opens in 1947 in Myrtle Beach, South Carolina. It is one of the earliest layouts along a sandy stretch dubbed the Grand Strand that will become a golf mecca.

MONSTER SLAYER

Prior to the 1951 U.S. Open at Oakland Hills, architect Robert Trent Jones Sr. gave the Detroit-area layout a menacing new look. Of particular concern for most players were narrowed fairways that left little room for error. Ben Hogan, like most of the players, balked at the changes, but he seemed to have little trouble on the par-70 track in Round 4. Hogan closed with a 67, the low round of the event, to win by two shots. Said Hogan: "I'm glad that I brought this course, this monster, to its knees."

Valley fever

Architect Dick Wilson completes Laurel Valley Country Club in Ligonier, Pennsylvania. The course is about 10 minutes from Latrobe Country Club, where Arnold Palmer learned to play the game. Palmer would become a member at Laurel Valley and spend years tinkering with Wilson's original layout.

NAME GAME

A fixture on the PGA Tour since 1962, the Blue Monster course at Doral Golf Resort & Spa in south Florida is built by real estate magnate Al Kaskell on drained swampland. The name Doral is a combination of "Al" and Kaskell's wife's name "Doris."

7,000 STRONG
THE NUMBER OF GOLF COURSES IN THE UNITED STATES
GROWS TO 7,000, AS STARS LIKE ARNOLD PALMER AND
JACK NICKLAUS MAKE THE GAME MORE APPEALING TO
THE MASSES.

OPEN PAIN
Unrelenting winds and a demanding
Championship Course at The Country Club
in Massachusetts takes its toll on the field at
the 1963 U.S. Open. Julius Boros wins the event
in a playoff with a 293 total, the highest winning
tally since 1935. Of 409 rounds played, only 14
are at or below par.

Crosby weather
Tony Lema struggles to a closing 76 in the
wind and rain to win the 1964 Bing Crosby Pro-
Am at Pebble Beach. Storms become such a
common theme at the event that players start
referring to the elements as "Crosby weather."

SUPERSTAR DESTROYER

San Francisco's Olympic Country Club has been the site of four U.S. Opens and more than its share of big-name collapses. In 1955, Jack Fleck stunned Ben Hogan on the rolling layout, and 11 years later Billy Casper edged Arnold Palmer in a playoff. The biggest surprise may have been the 1987 Open at Olympic, when Scott Simpson downed heavy favorite Tom Watson.

SPYGLASS HALF FULL

Although often overshadowed by its Monterey neighbors—Pebble Beach Golf Links and Cypress Point Club—many consider Spyglass Hill Golf Club in California almost as scenic and perhaps even more challenging. Spyglass Hill—a Robert Trent Jones Sr. design that opened in 1966—took its name from Robert Louis Stevenson's novel, *Treasure Island*. The course's holes are named after characters in the novel.

MUIRFIELD INFLUENCE

Jack Nicklaus won the 1966 British Open at Muirfield to complete the career Grand Slam. Nicklaus was so enamored with the Scottish layout, he modeled his home club in Ohio— Muirfield Village—after the design.

OAKMONT OVERWHELMS AMATEURS

Oakmont Country Club near Pittsburgh is so demanding during the 1969 U.S. Amateur only three players record rounds under par. Steve Melnyk wins with a 2-over 286 total.

NO SAFE HARBOUR

Although it will come to be known as a shot-makers course, when Harbour Town Golf Links debuts on the PGA Tour it is considered something of a brute. Arnold Palmer is the only player to break par at the first Heritage Golf Classic played on the South Carolina layout in 1969.

Unhappy at Hazeltine

Echoing the sentiments of most pros in the field at the 1970 U.S. Open, Dave Hill blasts Hazeltine National Golf Club in Minnesota after shooting a second-round 69. Hill says the only thing Hazeltine is missing is "80 acres of corn and a few cows." Hill finishes a distant second, seven strokes behind Tony Jacklin.

PINE VALLEY SOUTH

George Fazio's Jupiter Hills Club opens in 1970 in south Florida. The layout is routed through unkept sandy hills, much like Pine Valley in New Jersey, where Fazio formerly served as club professional.

IT'S A SMALL WORLD

Two of Walt Disney World's five resort courses open in 1971. The Joe Lee-designed Palm and Magnolia layouts will host the Magic Kingdom's PGA Tour event into the next century.

Quieting the Dog

Pete Dye's Teeth of the Dog layout at Casa de Campo in the Dominican Republic opens in 1971 with a whole new hazard for players to deal with. Before the nearby La Romana International Airport opened, a runway bisected two of the course's holes and often delayed play during takeoffs and landings.

HAVING A BALL ON THE BALGOVE

Not far from the hallowed turf of the Old Course at St. Andrews, Scotland, sits the Balgove course. The nine-hole, 1,520-yard course opened in 1972 and is designed for children. In fact, an adult can play the Balgove layout only if accompanied by a child.

USGA GIVES PEBBLE SOME PUNCH

Normally soggy and slow in January for the Bing Crosby National Pro-Am, Pebble Beach Golf Links plays hard and fast for June's U.S. Open in 1972. Jack Nicklaus, who also won that year's Crosby, wins the event with a 2-over 290 total and only 48 of the 150 starters score lower than 80 in Rounds 1 and 2.

TOUGH TIMES

In the early 1970s, Don January retires from competitive golf in order to focus on his budding golf course architecture business. But when business slows because of the recession that has gripped the nation, January returns to the PGA Tour in 1975. At age 45, he wins the 1975 San Antonio Open and the next year claims the Vardon Trophy for having the circuit's lowest scoring average.

SOMETHING SPECIAL AT SHINNECOCK

Fifty-five years after holding the first Walker Cup at The National Golf Links in New York, the USGA holds the 1977 matches at The National's posh neighbor; Shinnecock Hills. The event marks the first national tournament held on the exclusive layout since 1896, but it serves as a good warm-up. Shinnecock Hills would go on to host eight USGA championships, including four U.S. Opens.

STORM BREWING AT SHOAL CREEK

Shoal Creek Country Club in Alabama opens in 1977. The Jack Nicklaus design draws plenty of early accolades but prior to the 1990 PGA Championship becomes embroiled in a race controversy that becomes the club's lasting legacy.

PRICEY PEBBLE

IN 1979, 20TH CENTURY FOX FILM CORPORATION BUYS A COLLECTION OF MONTEREY PENINSULA GOLF PROPERTIES, INCLUDING PEBBLE BEACH GOLF LINKS, FOR $71 MILLION. TEN YEARS LATER, THE PROPERTIES ARE SOLD TO A JAPANESE COMPANY FOR $841 MILLION.

STADIUM SEATING

The Tournament Players Club at Sawgrass in Florida opens for play in 1980. PGA Tour commissioner Deane Beman purchases 415 acres of Florida swamp land for $1 and Pete Dye designs the first "Stadium" course, which features high mounding along fairways and around greens for galleries. The course becomes home of the PGA Tour's Tournament Players Championship.

A CUP WITH A VIEW

Although the Great Britain & Ireland team lose the 1981 Walker Cup, 15–9, they enjoy themselves along the way. The matches are played at Cypress Point Club in Pebble Beach. It's the only USGA event played on the scenic course.

DYE'S DEADLIEST

Billed as the world's most demanding layout, the Stadium Course at PGA West in California opens for play in 1986. The Pete Dye design quickly lives up to its reputation, and PGA Tour players have it removed from the rotation of the Bob Hope Classic after just one year.

A wet Western

The 1987 Western Open is washed out for two days by heavy rains. When play finally gets underway, nine holes on the adjacent Oak Brook Village Golf Club course are used because host-course Butler National is partially flooded.

IT'S ONLY MONEY

Although everything about Shadow Creek Golf Course is cloaked in secrecy, the cost to build the Tom Fazio design, which is located not far from "The Strip" in Las Vegas, is rumored to be $60 million. That's $20 million to build the course, $20 million for the landscaping, and $20 million for facilities. Predictably, the green fees are equally expensive. It costs $500 to play Shadow Creek, but you can only get a tee time if you're a guest at an MGM Mirage property, like the Bellagio or Mirage.

BEHIND THE IRON CURTAIN

The first golf course in the Soviet Union opens in 1989. The Tumba Golf Club is a nine-hole facility in Moscow.

Going long

PGA Tour rookie John Daly makes history with his victory at the 1991 PGA Championship at Crooked Stick Golf Club. The layout is a perfect fit for the hard-swinging but sometimes erratic Daly. It is the second longest course in PGA history with six par 4s over 440 yards and features wider-than-normal fairways for a major championship.

GLASS HALF EMPTY

THE 1996 AT&T PEBBLE BEACH NATIONAL PRO-AM IS CANCELED DUE TO FLOODING AT SPYGLASS HILL GOLF CLUB. IT MARKS THE FIRST TIME SINCE 1949 A PGA TOUR EVENT IS NOT COMPLETED BECAUSE OF WEATHER.

BANDON BRILLIANCE

In 1999, the first course opens at Bandon Dunes, a 1,200-acre golf resort on sandy bluffs overlooking the Pacific Ocean in Oregon. Designed by little-known architect David McLay Kidd, the rolling layout quickly ascends every golf course rating list. Two years later, Tom Doak ups the ante with his Pacific Dunes layout on the same site to make the craggy coastal area America's newest golf destination.

"PEOPLE'S OPEN"

Dubbed "The People's Open," the 2002 U.S. Open is the first held at a public golf course, Bethpage State Park's Black Course in New York. The A. W. Tillinghast-Joe Burbeck design also proves to be one of the championship's most demanding tracks. The 4-inch-deep bluegrass rough awaits wayward shots and some drives require carries of 250 yards or more. For New York residents, the pain is worth the price. Green fees for state residents are less than $40.

GOING THE DISTANCE

In an attempt to combat ever-increasing driving distance gains by players, architects have steadily lengthened courses. The 18th at Farmstead Golf Links in South Carolina is a par 6 that measures 767 yards. But that's just a warm-up for the 1,007-yard, par-6 ninth hole at Chocolay Downs Golf Course in Marquette, Michigan.

A SNAIL'S PACE

Doonbeg Golf Club opens in 2002 in County Clare, Ireland, to plenty of fanfare, but the routing wasn't what architect Greg Norman had originally envisioned. A tiny endangered species of snail had been discovered living in the soil along the dunes of Doughmore Bay, so the course had to be rerouted.

LICENSE TO COMPLAIN

The hardest thing for a modern golf course architect to do is please a touring professional. Pros are notoriously opinionated when it comes to the courses they play. Jack Nicklaus, the game's all-time major champion and respected architect, once lambasted the TPC of Sawgrass in Florida. He harshly criticized the setup and likened some of its approach shots to "stopping a 5-iron on the hood of a car." Lee Trevino once asked of Riviera Country Club's seventh hole: "What happened to the other half of the fairway?" Few players, however, were as creative as pro journeyman John Maginnes when he assessed Orange Country National in Florida, site of the 2003 PGA Tour Qualifying School Tournament. "I like golf courses with a little subtlety to them. These two courses are like two fall-down drunks sitting in a New York bar."

Straits shooter

More so than any of the other governing bodies of golf's four majors—Augusta National, U.S. Golf Association, and the Royal & Ancient Golf Club—the PGA of America embraces change. It's that adventurous spirit that led the association to host the 2004 PGA Championship at Whistling Straits in Wisconsin. Built on land that was once a U.S. Army base on the shores of Lake Michigan, the 7-year-old Pete Dye design was the longest in major championship history at 7,536 yards. "What a great monster you've created here," said champion Vijay Singh.

TRUMP CARD

Built on the 500-acre estate of former automaker John DeLorean in New Jersey, Trump National Golf Club opens in 2004. The layout was designed by Tom Fazio and the clubhouse is located in the failed carmaker's mansion.

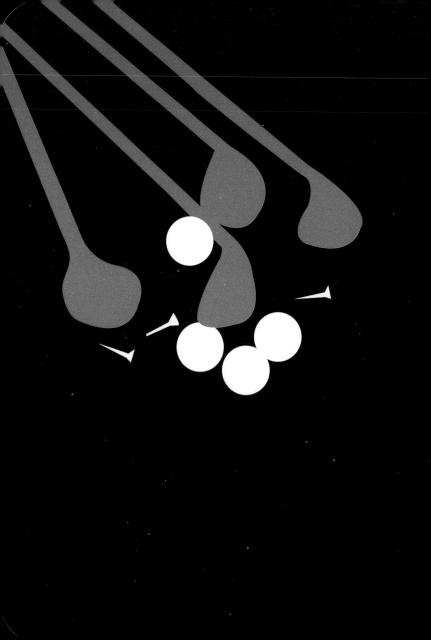

Implements & impediments

"Golf is a game whose aim is to hit a very small ball into an even smaller hole, with weapons singularly ill-designed for the purpose."
Winston Churchill

OF KINGS AND CLUBS
In 1603, King James I of England and VI of Scotland names Edinburgh bow maker William Mayne the first "royal clubmaker."

No game for the masses

The earliest clubs feature clubheads made of beech, holly, pear, or apple wood, which are connected to the shafts using a splint and then bound tightly using leather straps. Because these early models have a tendency to crack, a golfer can expect to break at least one club per round, meaning the game is much too expensive for most people to play.

A FEATHERIE FUTURE

In its earliest days, the game was played with hard wooden golf balls that flew erratically and were expensive to make. In 1618, the feather golf ball or "Featherie" is introduced. Several pieces of leather are stitched together, leaving a small opening. The ball is then stuffed with a top-hatful of feathers that have been boiled and softened. The ball is then pounded into shape.

AN EARLY ARTIST

HUGH PHILP IS APPOINTED CLUBMAKER TO THE SOCIETY OF ST. ANDREWS GOLFERS (LATER THE ROYAL AND ANCIENT GOLF CLUB) IN 1819. PHILP IS ONE OF THE MOST RENOWNED OF THE EARLY LONG-NOSED CLUBMAKERS.

HICKORY HISTORY

Scottish clubmaker Robert Forgan, who was Hugh Philp's nephew, begins using hickory for his golf shafts in 1826. The hickory is imported from the United States and replaces ash and hazel, which had been used previously. In 1863, Forgan becomes clubmaker to the Prince of Wales, later Edward VII.

LONG-DRIVE KING

In 1836, Samuel Messieux records the longest drive using a featherie ball. Messieux launches a 361-yard shot at Elysian Fields, but there's a catch—the drive is downwind and on frozen ground.

GETTING OUT OF A RUT

Because the featherie ball has a tendency to become damaged when hit by the early irons, most players favor using a wide range of wooden clubs. One exception is the "rutting iron," which is used when a ball comes to rest in a cartwheel rut.

GUTTA PERCHA REVOLUTION

The Reverend Roger Paterson introduces the gutta percha, or "guttie," golf ball in 1848. The guttie is made from the sap of a rubber tree known as a gutta percha. The new ball flies much farther and costs less than a featherie, which could be more expensive than a golf club.

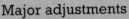

Major adjustments

The Urquhart adjustable-head club debuts in 1895. The new club allows the angle of the clubhead to be altered to suit the shot. Other clubmakers create clubs with detachable heads that allow a player to carry a single shaft and attach whichever head they need for a particular shot.

TEEING OFF

George F. Grant—a Harvard graduate, dentist, inventor, and son of former slaves—patents a wooden tee in 1899. Prior to Grant's invention, players used sand or dirt to prop the ball up for driving.

Technology takes center stage

While many consider the current spate of technological advancements in golf equipment the greatest the game has ever seen, at the turn of the 19th century golf celebrated a trio of inventive breakthroughs. In 1900, W. M. Mollison invents and patents the perforated leather grip for golf clubs. The same year, clubmakers make Alghou persimmon the material of choice for clubheads. Prior to 1900, beech and other hardwoods had been used. In 1901, A. T. Saunders patents a golf ball with a compressed-air center. The air is injected into the ball with a hypodermic needle.

BIGGER NOT ALWAYS BETTER

The period between 1900–1930 features hundreds of innovations in golf club design, but few are as outlandish as the "giant niblicks." Some of the oversized wedges measure over six inches across, but few are used by the best players.

"BOUNDING BILLY"

Perhaps the greatest breakthrough in golf ball technology occurred at the turn of the century in Cleveland, Ohio. Coburn Haskell, with some help from Bertram Work who lived in nearby Akron, experiments with a ball made of rubber thread wound around a solid rubber core. The gutta-percha cover of Haskell's original ball was smooth, which at first causes the ball to fly erratically, earning it the nickname "Bounding Billy." A bramble pattern is used to give the new ball aerodynamic stability. The "Haskell"—as it comes to be called—is an immediate success. Walter Travis uses it to win the 1901 U.S. Amateur Championship and, by 1902, nearly all the major championships are won by players using the new ball with a dimple-patterned cover.

Sandwich sensation

With a little help from a friend, Walter Travis becomes the first foreigner to win the British Amateur title in 1904. When the Australian-born Travis arrives at Sandwich for the championship, he is struggling so badly on the course's greens that a friend suggests he try the center-shafted Schenectady putter. Travis is barely challenged on his way to victory using the revolutionary new club.

A NEW SPIN

England's E. Burr quietly revolutionizes the use of irons when he receives a patent for "rib-faced" clubs. The horizontal channels impart much-needed backspin on golf balls, a particularly useful result at courses where greens are hard and fast.

DIMPLE DESTINY

Throughout the early history of golf ball design there was no shortage of cover designs aimed at creating the optimal aerodynamic pattern. In 1905, William Taylor discovers a concave dimple pattern that he patents. The dimple design quickly proves superior to the preferred bramble cover that is in use at the time. Shortly after Taylor's discovery, A. G. Spalding unveils his company's first dimpled golf ball.

ALL HOT AIR

Arthur Smith was one of the first players to win a major championship (1905 Western Open) using a pneumatic golf ball. The pneumatic balls feature a hard-rubber shell filled with compressed air. The only problem? Many of the pneumatic golf balls, like the version made by Goodyear Tire and Rubber Co., tend to explode in hot weather.

A ROUGH RAKE

In 1905, James Ross Brown introduces the "rake iron." The club face resembles the teeth in a comb and is designed to help players hit from deep rough.

PRICEY PELLETS

For all modern golfers who balk at a $50 price tag for a dozen, high-performance golf balls, consider the price golfers used to pay for a dozen Spaldings. In 1906, the company introduces its "Dot" line for the exorbitant price—at least at the time—of $6 a dozen.

Laying down the law

The first reference to equipment in the Rules of Golf occurs in 1908. The Royal and Ancient Golf Club of St. Andrews—which sets the standard for clubs in the United Kingdom—declares that a club must be comprised of "a plain shaft and a head that does not contain any mechanical contrivance, such as springs." In 1910, the R&A bans the use of center-shafted putters, like the one used by Walter Travis to win the 1904 British Amateur. The decision creates a split with the U.S. Golf Association that lasts until 1952.

Good Knight

In 1910, Arthur Knight obtains a patent for a seamed, tubular steel golf shaft. Until then, shafts have been made from various types of wood, including ash, hazel, and hickory.

HELPFUL HINTS

In 1911, H. Cawsey patents the first reminder grip, which features a ridge on the side of the handle opposite the clubhead designed to help players grip the club properly.

Groovey debate begins

Early golf club visionary Willie Park Jr. introduces the "stepped-face" iron in 1913, which features a series of deep grooves. The grooves allow players to spin golf balls more effectively and thus control their approach shots. Some claim that the grooves make the game too easy, sparking a debate that will continue throughout the century.

TEMPER, TEMPER

Golf clubs usually pay the price for a shot poorly played. Breaking, throwing, and destroying golf clubs is a common sight at every level of the game. Even the game's quintessential gentleman, Bobby Jones, wasn't above the occasional toss after a bad shot. Following a heated first-round match against Eben Byers at the 1916 U.S. Amateur Championship, which featured plenty of club throwing, Jones quipped: "We both showed our tempers out there, and I only won because he ran out of clubs first."

GOOD BUSINESS

Tom Auchterlonie opens an equipment shop in 1919 less than 100 yards from the Old Course's 18th green in St. Andrews, Scotland. The store is still in business to this day.

"Calamity Jane"

By the time Bobby Jones was given the simple offset blade putter that would gain a place in golf lore, it was 20 years old and already nicknamed "Calamity Jane." Jones replaced the original Calamity Jane with a duplicate in 1926 that was made by Spalding and known as Calamity Jane II. The original Calamity Jane is at Augusta National Golf Club in Georgia, while Calamity Jane II was donated to the USGA Museum.

THE SECRET'S OUT

Long before equipment endorsements became big business, the major golf ball manufacturers met in 1928 and agreed not to pay pros secret salaries for using their brand in competition.

A true step foreward

In February 1929, True Temper Co. patents a seamless, steel shaft with a stepdown taper that will become the industry standard. The steel shaft allows for mass production, which is followed by the numbering of clubs. Numbers replace the names for clubs like brassie (modern 2-wood), spoon (3-wood), cleek (4-wood), baffy (5-wood), mashie (5-iron), and niblick (9-iron).

R&A ENTERS STEEL AGE

A few months too late to help the U.S. Ryder Cup team, which had to revert back to hickory shafts for the 1929 matches held in England, the Royal and Ancient Golf Club approves the use of steel-shafted clubs in its championships. Reportedly, the move by the R&A is prompted by the Prince of Wales, who uses steel-shafted clubs to play the Old Course at St. Andrews in 1929.

A GRAND SAND WEDGE

Using a new concave-faced sand wedge that will be deemed illegal by the U.S. Golf Association in 1931, Bobby Jones wins the 1930 British Open for the second leg of the Grand Slam.

USGA changes course

Following Billy Burke's victory at the 1931 U.S. Open using the "balloon" golf ball (1.55 ounces in weight, 1.68 inches in diameter), the U.S. Golf Association adopts a new weight limit (1.62 ounces) for all golf balls, starting in 1932. The R&A maintains its 1.62 inch and 1.62 ounce limits.

SARAZEN'S NEW WEAPON

Prior to the 1932 British Open, Gene Sarazen came up with an idea that would make it easier to play from sand traps. Sarazen solders lead onto the back of his most lofted club. The bellylike flange kept the club from digging into the sand. At the 1932 Open, which Sarazen won by five strokes, he is so concerned that officials will ban the club, he hides it under his coat each night and sneaks it to his room. "I showed the club to the people at Wilson and they began making them right away. Since I was under contract with [Wilson], I never made a nickel off my idea," Sarazen recalls years later.

A NEW SPIN

In October 1935, Dr. John Monteith Jr. creates a "mechanical niblick" (9-iron) to test how a spinning golf ball reacts to different types of grasses.

Thinner thinking

A new steel shaft debuts in 1935 with a thinner tip and increased flexibility that reportedly increases clubhead speed by 21 percent. The shaft wholesales for $4.80.

BOUNCE BACK

CONCERNED THAT THE MODERN GOLF BALL HAD BECOME TOO LIVELY, IN JULY 1936 THE ROYAL AND ANCIENT GOLF CLUB INVITES MANUFACTURERS TO PRODUCE "SLOWER" GOLF BALLS.

Hickory's last stand

John Fischer beats Jack McLean on the first extra hole in the final match to win the 1936 U.S. Amateur, and become the last player to win a USGA championship using hickory-shafted clubs.

A FULL BAG

Starting in 1938, the USGA announces players will be limited to 14 clubs in their bags during a round. Four days after the USGA decree, the R&A rejects the club limit, creating a split between golf's ruling bodies.

THE FIX IS OFF

In March 1938, the U.S. Federal Trade Commission orders eight golf equipment manufacturers and the PGA of America to stop golf ball price-fixing.

DISTANCE UP FOR DEBATE

Ever-improving golf ball technology prompts the USGA to begin a program in 1939 to "stabilize" the golf ball at its current maximum distance.

War halts golf ball production

In December 1941, the U.S. Office of Price Administration reduces the production of new golf balls by 80 percent in an attempt to conserve rubber supplies. Less than four months later, the manufacture of all golf balls is halted. By 1944, the golf ball shortage is so acute that Gene Sarazen urges players to reprocess their old balls or "next year you'll be swinging at potatoes."

WAR RELIEF

With golf balls so scarce that top pros are paying up to $4 for a pre-war ball, the government eases restrictions on manufacturers in early 1945. Companies are allowed to make golf balls with synthetic rubber cores.

A LOFTY DEBUT

THE FIRST MACHINE THAT CAN ADJUST A CLUB'S LOFT AND LIE IS MARKETED BY ADJUSTO-MATIC CO. IN 1955. THE DEVICE IS CALLED THE SAM SNEAD ADJUSTO-MATIC.

FORGING AHEAD

The casting method of manufacturing clubheads is introduced in 1963. Although this makes clubs more affordable, professionals continue to use hand-forged clubs because of the increased feel and control.

SOLHEIM STARTS SMALL

Working in his Redwood City, California garage, mechanical engineer Karsten Solheim creates the 1-A putter in 1959 and launches the Ping brand.

WHITE FANG

Prior to the 1967 U.S. Open, Jack Nicklaus adds a new putter to his bag. It is a white-painted, bull's-eye flat stick that Nicklaus affectionately calls "White Fang." The new putter causes Nicklaus to slightly alter his putting stroke. With White Fang, Nicklaus wins his second Open and tops the scoring record with a 275 total.

Top of the world
In 1972, Spalding introduces the Top-Flite golf ball, the first two-piece ball with a durable cover.

GOING GRAPHITE
The graphite shaft debuts in 1973. The space-age material offers rigidity, lightness, and increased strength over steel shafts.

A size standard
After decades of debate, the R&A and USGA finally agree to a standard-sized golf ball in 1973. The 1.68 inch, 1.55 ounce ball is agreed upon for all competitions. Prior to 1973, the R&A favors a smaller ball (1.62 inch), but in 1974 the organization makes the larger ball compulsory for the British Open.

 THE GOLF GEEK'S BIBLE

TRANSMITTER STATIC

A golf ball built with a small transmitter inside that allows a player to use a radio receiver to locate the ball debuts in 1973. Both the R&A and USGA promptly ban its use in competitions.

A 5-wood future

During a time when most pros use 4-woods, Raymond Floyd trades the traditional club for a more lofted 5-wood prior to the 1976 Masters. The club allows Floyd to attack Augusta National's par-5 holes, which he plays in 14 under par, and win his only Masters. Following Floyd's victory, the 5-wood becomes a popular item among Tour pros.

BLACK KNIGHTED

In his prime, Gary Player is considered one of the game's greatest putters—a skill that helps lead the Black Knight to nine major titles, the last coming in 1978 at the Masters. Player, like most good putters, is extremely protective of his putter. He may, however, have taken it a bit too far when he said: "If I had to choose between my wife and my putter, I'd sure miss her."

HEAVY METAL

TaylorMade Golf introduces its first metal wood in March 1979. Many pros balk at the club at first, but it signals a new era in the equipment industry.

LEVI LEAVES HIS MARK

Wayne Levi wins the 1982 Hawaiian Open, to become the first player to claim a PGA Tour title with an orange-colored golf ball. Jerry Pate would quickly follow Levi's lead, winning that year's Tournament Players Championship with an orange ball.

"LITTLE BEN"

Two-time Masters champion Ben Crenshaw is a renowned putter thanks to a $20 investment by his father. Throughout his career, Crenshaw used a Wilson 8802 blade putter—nicknamed "Little Ben"—that was bought for him by his father from a Texas pro shop when Crenshaw was a boy. "That club's been the best provider in the family," Crenshaw's father, Charlie, wrote in the book *Texas Golf Legends*.

GOING LONG

CHARLES OWENS WINS THE 1986 TREASURE COAST CLASSIC TO BECOME THE FIRST PLAYER TO WIN A SENIOR PGA TOUR EVENT USING A LONG PUTTER.

PECULIAR PUTTERS

More so than any other club, putters often feature the most interesting designs. Two-time Masters champion Bernhard Langer has used a putter that had three plastic balls attached in line behind the head. And Jack Nicklaus won the 1986 Masters with a putter that resembled a vacuum cleaner.

LOVE ENDS LONG WAIT

One of the final metalwood holdouts gives in to technology in 1997. Davis Love III trades in his old Cleveland Golf wood-headed driver, which he's used since joining the PGA Tour in 1985, for a new metal-headed driver. Fittingly, Love wins his first major (PGA Championship) in 1997. "I'd tried it (metal-headed driver) but then gave it to someone else on the range. And then he started bombing it, so I grabbed it back from him and just started using it," Love said.

ALL EYES ON PING EYE 2S

Karsten Manufacturing rekindles the groove debate in 1987 when the PGA Tour and USGA declare the grooves in the company's new Ping Eye 2 Irons don't conform to the Rules of Golf. The Tour and USGA claim the grooves are too close together, but Karsten will challenge the ruling in court. In a compromise, the USGA allows the irons in its competitions until 1990 and the clubs continue to be legal until 1996.

TOUR TAKES A STANCE

In early 1989, the PGA Tour bans square-grooved irons beginning in the 1990 season. In December, a federal judge grants Karsten Manufacturing, maker of the Ping clubs that sparked the dispute, an injunction to stop the Tour's ban pending the outcome of the company's lawsuit against the Tour.

ALL SQUARE

The USGA and Karsten Manufacturing settle their grooves dispute out of court in January 1990. The USGA rules the Ping irons are legal, but future clubs must conform to groove-width standards.

CALLAWAY MAKES BIG BREAKTHROUGH

Callaway Golf Co. introduces the Big Bertha driver in early 1991. Named after a World War I artillery piece, the Big Bertha is the first metal wood with an oversized head. "We're betting a big part of our future on the Big Bertha," said company founder Ely Callaway. The driver becomes one of the game's most successful-selling clubs. In 1990, Callaway posts net sales of $21.5 million; by 1997, net sales had grown to $842.9 million.

The softer side of golf

In 1993, Bill Ward, a Jackson, Wyoming, golf course owner, purchases the rights to a soft, rubber golf cleat and soon launches Softspikes Inc. Although Softspikes are slow to catch on, particularly among pros who favor the old metal spikes, the green-friendly alternatives eventually earn mainstream appeal. By 2000, about 7,500 U.S. golf courses have banned metal spikes and the soft cleats have become the rule, rather than the exception.

DODGING BULLETS

IN 1994, BULLET GOLF FILES A $20 MILLION LAWSUIT AGAINST THE USGA FOR BANNING ITS HOLLOW POINT DRIVER AND MAGNIFICENT 7 METALWOOD. THE ASSOCIATION DEEMS BOTH CLUBS NONCONFORMING.

HOPE SPRINGS ETERNAL

In early 1995, "spring-like effect" enters the golf lexicon as drivers with thin metal faces come into vogue. The rebound of the ball off these "hot" faces causes pros and amateurs to gain distance with their tee shots.

HAVING A BALL

While "hot faced" drivers dominate equipment news in 1995, the new year brings a spate of new golf ball technology. In 1996, Spalding unveils the Strata, the company's first multi-layer, non-wound golf ball. In the same year, Precept introduces the MC Tour, the first three-piece, non-wound ball with a urethane cover.

Limits looming

In June 1998, the USGA proposes a conformance test for springlike effect, or rebound effect, in drivers. Although all existing drivers are expected to conform, many manufacturers blast the test protocol at a forum in September. Despite the outcry, the USGA enacts the testing. The USGA sets the limit for coefficient of restitution, or COR, at .830. In 2000, the organization releases a list of banned drivers that includes the new Callaway ERC.

A SIZABLE DEBATE

When Callaway Golf introduces its first Big Bertha driver in early 1991, the "oversized" clubhead measures 195 cubic centimeters. In 2004, the USGA moves to limit clubhead size, creating a 460cc maximum. The USGA also limits shaft sizes to 48 inches for all clubs except putters.

BELLY UP
PAUL AZINGER SPARKS A TREND ON THE PGA TOUR IN 1999 WHEN HE STARTS USING A TRIMMED-DOWN LONG PUTTER, WHICH HE ANCHORS AGAINST HIS BELLY.

COMING UNWOUND
The Titleist Pro V1—a solid golf ball that features a high-energy core and a soft urethane cover—officially debuts at the 2000 Invensys Classic in Las Vegas. Billy Andrade wins the event and signals the end of the wound ball era.

KEEPING AN EYE ON THE BALL
In an April 2005 letter, the USGA requests a handful of golf ball manufacturers to submit prototype golf balls that fly 15 and 25 yards shorter. Many view the letter as a first step in the process to scale back how far modern golf balls travel.

A cup full

"This whole team and also myself, we just live for this."

Spain's Sergio García after Europe's victory at the 2004 Ryder Cup

CURTIS CUP PRECURSOR

In 1905, a first-of-its-kind team match between the top women golfers from Great Britain and the United States was held. The British team easily won, 6–1, but the event laid the foundation for what would become the Curtis Cup.

FEATHER IN HER CAP

In an attempt to spur interest in an international women's team event, Margaret and Harriot Curtis—who clashed in the final match of the 1907 U.S. Women's Amateur Championship—travel to England. Unfortunately, Margaret steals the spotlight with her signature feathered hats.

BRITISH LADIES SPURN U.S. OFFER

The British Ladies Golf Union balks at a proposal by the U.S. Golf Association to donate a cup for an international women's team competition. The British organization says it would be too difficult to select a team.

PORTRUSH PRECURSOR

A team match called "American and Colonial versus Great Britain" is held in 1911 at Portrush Golf Club. The amateur event is won by Great Britain, 7–2.

LACK OF INTEREST

Just two Americans, Bobby Jones and Max Marston, volunteer to play for the 1920 Olympic team, prompting officials to cancel the squad's trip to the games in Belgium.

Walker up to challenge

U.S. Golf Association president George Herbert Walker donates the International Challenge Trophy in 1921. The event is originally open to any country that can field an amateur team, but the press dubs the trophy the Walker Cup and the match eventually becomes a competition between the United States and Great Britain & Ireland. The first match is played in August 1922 at National Golf Links of America in New York and, surprisingly, is won by the U.S., 8–4.

DARWIN'S BIG MOMENT

Renowned golf writer Bernard Darwin travels to the inaugural Walker Cup Match in 1922 in New York to cover the event for *The Times* of London, but when Great Britain & Ireland captain Robert Harris becomes ill and must withdraw from the competition, Darwin steps in as the team's playing captain. Darwin defeats U.S. captain William C. Fownes Jr., 3 and 1, in their singles match, but it is the U.S. team, which includes Chick Evans and Bobby Jones, that easily wins the event, 8–4.

MONEY MATTERS

THE UNITED STATES EXTENDS ITS UNDEFEATED STREAK TO 3–0 AT THE 1924 WALKER CUP IN NEW YORK, BUT BECAUSE OF FINANCIAL CONSTRAINTS ORGANIZERS DECIDE TO HOLD THE EVENT EVERY OTHER YEAR.

Brits win Ryder Cup warm-up

In what is a prelude to the inaugural Ryder Cup, a team of British professionals thump their U.S. counterparts, 13½–1½, in 1926 at Wentworth, England.

PLANTING THE SEEDS OF SUCCESS

Samuel Ryder, an English seed merchant who supplied golf courses in the United States and Great Britain, donates the trophy in 1927 for the first professional team matches between the U.S. and Great Britain. Ryder paid £250 for the 17-inch-high trophy.

CAPTAIN HAIG

Riding the momentum of captain Walter Hagen's play, the 1927 U.S. Ryder Cup team wins the first Ryder Cup, 9½–2½, at Worcester Country Club in Massachusetts. Hagen easily wins his singles match, 2 and 1, over Arthur Havers to complete a year that included The Haig's fourth consecutive PGA Championship and his fourth Western Open title.

SISTER SALUTE

Harriott Curtis and her sister Margaret donate a cup for a proposed match between amateur ladies from the United States and Great Britain, but the U.S. Golf Association withholds acceptance.

Jones in charge

First-time captain Bobby Jones leads the 1928 U.S. Walker Cup team to victory, 11–1, at Chicago Golf Club. Jones also sets the margin for most lopsided 36-hole singles match, beating Phil Perkins, 13 and 12.

AT HOME WITH HICKORY THE BRITS PREVAIL

Although the U.S. side was heavily favored to win the 1929 Ryder Cup, the Great Britain team had two advantages. For the first time the matches were being played in England, at Moortown Golf Club, and because the Royal and Ancient Golf Club had not yet approved the use of steel shafts in golf clubs, the American side would have to revert back to hickory shafts for the event. After falling behind on Day 1, 2½–1½, Great Britain rallies to win five of the eight singles matches and claim the Cup.

Grand beginning

A week before embarking on his quest for the Grand Slam, Bobby Jones leads the 1930 U.S. Walker Cup team to victory, 10–2, at Royal St. George's in England. The United States remains undefeated in the matches.

GOOD GOLLY MISS MOLLY

Led by Molly Gourlay, a team of lady British amateurs edge their American counterparts, 8½–6½, in 1930 at Sunningdale, England. The public embraces the match, which ensures the debut of the Curtis Cup two years later.

RYDER CUP ROW

The United States sails to a 9–3 victory at the 1931 Ryder Cup largely because of three key no-shows for Great Britain. Percy Alliss and Aubrey Boomer were not allowed to compete because they both lived outside of Great Britain, and Henry Cotton was officially barred because he wanted to travel separately from the team.

GB&I cruises at first Curtis Cup

With the USGA's backing, the first Curtis Cup is played in 1932 in Wentworth, England. The Great Britain & Ireland team wins the one-day event, 5½–3½.

MORE RYDER CUP RUMBLINGS

In what will be the last Ryder Cup that namesake Samuel Ryder will attend, the Great Britain side withstands a furious final-day rally by the Americans to reclaim the chalice in 1933. The victory will be Great Britain's last for 24 years.

CONFIDENCE KILLS

Following the team's inspiring victory at the 1933 Ryder Cup, a confident British team insures the Cup for its return to England when they travel to the U.S. for the 1935 matches. Led by Walter Hagen, who in five Ryder Cups posted a 7–1–1 record, the Americans rolled to a convincing 9–3 victory.

No tie for GB&I

The United States and Great Britain & Ireland play to a 4½–4½ draw at the third Curtis Cup in 1936. However, the British team declines to share the Cup, contending they had not won any claim to it.

AN AMERICAN SHUTOUT

ALTHOUGH THE GREAT BRITAIN & IRELAND SIDE SALVAGES THREE HALVES, THEY FAIL TO WIN A FULL POINT AND THE UNITED STATES ROMPS TO A 9–0 VICTORY IN THE 1936 WALKER CUP. THE ROUT MARKS THE ONLY SHUTOUT IN MATCH HISTORY.

TRANSATLANTIC BREAKTHROUGH

In what will be the final Ryder Cup before World War II, the United States wins its first match on English soil at the 1937 matches. America's Ralph Guldahl leads the U.S. effort, going 2–0 with an 8-and-7 pummeling of Alf Padgham in singles play.

TENTH TIME'S A CHARM

At home on the hard, ancient turf of St. Andrews, Scotland, Great Britain & Ireland ends its winless run at the 1938 Walker Cup. GB&I stuns the U.S. squad, 7–4. The GB&I turnaround is credited to John Beck—an outgoing and energetic captain who held trial matches in the spring of 1938 in an attempt to build team harmony.

CUP CANCELLATIONS

With the onset of World War II, the 1939 Ryder Cup as well as subsequent Curtis and Walker Cups are canceled. Charles Roe, the secretary of Great Britain's PGA, informs his American counterpart of the cancellation via a telegram: "When we have settled our differences and peace reigns, we will see that our team comes across to remove the Ryder Cup from your safekeeping." The next five U.S. Ryder Cup teams (1939–1943) play exhibition matches that raise funds for the Red Cross and United Service Organizations (USO).

BRITAIN'S CUP STILL HALF FULL

The British PGA denies a U.S. request to resume the Ryder Cup in 1945. Great Britain is still reeling from World War II and won't be able to field a team for two years, and only then through the financial help of Robert Hudson, an Oregon fruit grower.

CHANGE OF SCENERY CAN'T SLOW U.S.

Because of travel constraints on the Great Britain & Ireland team, the 1947 Walker Cup is held in Scotland, instead of the United States where it was originally slated to be played. The change of venue does little to deter the Americans, who reclaim the Cup with an 8–4 victory.

PORTLAND POUNDING

Americans Lew Worsham and Porky Oliver score one of the most lopsided victories in Ryder Cup history—a 10-and-9 foursomes romp—as the U.S. side easily defeats a beleaguered Great Britain & Ireland team at the 1947 matches. The only highlight for GB&I is Sam King's scrappy victory in the final singles match to avoid a U.S. shutout.

HOGAN BLOWS WHISTLE ON BRITISH GROOVES

In what many considered retaliation for an incident at the 1947 Ryder Cup, non-competing U.S. captain Ben Hogan stirs the pre-match waters in 1949 when he complains about the grooves on the clubs of some British players. An R&A inspection shows some of the British clubs were non-conforming and Jock Ballantine, the pro at the host club in England, spends the night before the matches grinding the grooves to conformity. At the 1947 Ryder Cup, Henry Cotton had officials inspect Hogan's clubs. No illegal grooves were found.

WINLESS AT WINGED FOOT

IN THE FIRST WALKER CUP PLAYED IN THE UNITED STATES SINCE 1936, A TALENTED AMERICAN SQUAD AND A TAXING LAYOUT PROVE TO BE TOO MUCH FOR THE GB&I SIDE AT THE 1949 MATCHES. AFTER TAKING A COMMANDING 3–1 LEAD ON DAY 1, THE AMERICANS WIN SEVEN OF THE EIGHT SINGLES MATCHES AT WINGED FOOT IN NEW YORK TO EASILY RETAIN THE CUP.

SHORT-HANDED

Without the services of Ben Hogan, who is still recovering from a horrific car accident, and reigning U.S. Open champion Cary Middlecoff, who was not a member of the PGA and therefore not eligible to play in the Ryder Cup, the United States ekes out a 7–5 victory over Great Britain & Ireland in 1949 at Ganton Golf Club in England.

Close call

In the most closely contested Walker Cup yet, the United States pulls out a 6–3 victory in 1951 at Royal Birkdale in England. Despite the final outcome, the Great Britain & Ireland side pushes the U.S. to the limit, with three of the foursomes matches being decided on the final hole.

U.S. PERFECT AT PINEHURST

In the event's only visit to the legendary No. 2 Course at Pinehurst, the United States defeats the Great Britain & Ireland side in the 1951 Ryder Cup. Only two of the 12 singles matches reach the 18th hole, with the U.S. winning all but one. Particularly inspiring was Skip Alexander's performance at the matches. Alexander, who just two months earlier returned to competition after being badly injured in a plane crash, cruises to an 8-and-7 triumph over John Panton.

FEELING THE HEAT

The 1953 Ryder Cup provides a glimpse of what the pressure-filled matches would become. Great Britain rallies early on the second day, winning three of the first four singles matches. However, the tide turns when Peter Alliss chunks his chip on the 18th green on his way to a double bogey and a 1-up loss, and Bernard Hunt three-putts the last hole to slip into a tie with Dave Douglas. The U.S. holds on for a 6½–5½ victory.

SUMMER BLUES

The weather was so warm during practice rounds for the 1953 Walker Cup at The Kittansett Club in Massachusetts that members of the GB&I team, who didn't pack shorts, simply cut their trousers off at the knees. On the course, however, it was the American putters that sizzled as the home team cruises to a 9–3 rout.

SWEET SWEEP

THE UNITED STATES, LED BY U.S. WOMEN'S AMATEUR
CHAMPION BARBARA ROMACK, SWEEPS THE FOURSOMES
MATCHES TO REGAIN THE CURTIS CUP AT THE 1954
MATCHES.

A FORMIDABLE FOURSOME

*A 1955 U.S. Ryder Cup team that features
five rookies gets a boost by the play of
Tommy Bolt, Jack Burke Jr., Doug Ford, and
Sam Snead. The foursome enjoy two victories
apiece and account for all of the American
points. The U.S. eases to an 8–4 conquest.*

WALK-OVER CUP

Drummed thoroughly in foursomes play, 4–0, the
GB&I team falls to the United States, 10–2, at the
1955 Walker Cup. The matches are dubbed the
"Walk-over Cup" and GB&I captain Alec Hill
is particularly criticized by the British media.
Years after the match, Hill said the only way he'd
captain another team was if "… no one on the
team would be allowed to read newspapers
(during the matches)."

PRINCELY CONCLUSION

Great Britain & Ireland nips the United States in the 1956 Curtis Cup at Prince's Golf Club in England. The victory is the GB&I side's second in the last three matches.

Dangerous duo

In the 1956 Canada Cup, a two-man event for professionals, American legends Ben Hogan and Sam Snead combine for a 14-stroke victory. The U.S. will win eight of the 14 Canada Cups. In 1967, the event becomes the World Cup.

GREAT BRITAIN BOUNCES BACK

Rejuvenated by a new selection system and an influx of funding from Sir Stuart Goodwin, who donates £10,000 ($18,134) to the team, Great Britain stages a furious final-day rally to win the 1957 Ryder Cup. The British side wins six of the eight singles games to win its first match in 24 years.

Close, but no cup

The United States' domination of the Walker Cup begins to ebb at the 1957 matches. The U.S. lead 2–1 after day 1 and at one point on the final day the match is all square. But a furious comeback by William Patton over Reid Jack in the singles helps turn the tide for the Americans. "At about three o'clock this afternoon I thought the Walker Cup was half-way across the Atlantic," said U.S. captain Charles Coe at the closing ceremony.

NEW WORLD ORDER

The Great Britain & Ireland team plays the U.S. side to a draw, 4½–4½, at the 1958 Curtis Cup at Brae Burn Country Club in Massachusetts. The showing is the team's best on American soil and allows them to retain the Cup.

TURBULENT TIMES

In an ominous start to Great Britain's attempt to win back-to-back Ryder Cup matches for the first time, the team's flight from Los Angeles to Palm Springs, California, must return to L.A. airport after experiencing severe turbulence. Instead of taking a later flight, the team arrives at the 1959 matches by bus. Things don't get any easier for Great Britain, however, the U.S. team loses just two matches and rolls to an 8½–3½ victory.

WEST COAST WEARY

In 1961, the Walker Cup is played on the United States' West Coast for the first time. The added travel seems to have an effect on the GB&I team, which falls to the United States 11–1 in the event's most lopsided outcome thus far. This is the last match to be contested over 36 holes. In an attempt to close the gap between the U.S. and GB&I, additional foursome and singles series are added and all matches are reduced to 18-hole "sprints."

ARNIE ACES DEBUT

Arnold Palmer goes 3–0–1 in his Ryder Cup debut to help lead the United States to an easy victory in the 1961 matches. Palmer's play helps make up for the loss of Sam Snead, who is barred from the matches by the PGA because he played in an unsanctioned event, the Portland Open.

Bearless, but still the best

Even without Jack Nicklaus, who isn't eligible because he hasn't completed his PGA apprenticeship, the United States sails to a 23–9 victory at the 1963 Ryder Cup. Before the matches, playing captain Arnold Palmer boldly announces: "This team would beat the rest of the world combined."

CUP CONTROL

The United States continues its stranglehold on the Walker Cup, downing the GB&I side, 12–8, in the 1963 matches. The Americans hold a 18–1 advantage in the series and haven't lost since 1938.

Two of a kind

Normally foes on the golf course, Jack Nicklaus and Arnold Palmer prove to be as prolific as a team as they are as individuals. The two team up to win the 1963, '64, '66, and '67 Canada Cups.

A TIE WORTH CHEERING

THE UNITED STATES AND GREAT BRITAIN & IRELAND PLAY TO AN 11–11 TIE AT THE 1965 WALKER CUP AT BALTIMORE (MARYLAND) COUNTRY CLUB. ALTHOUGH THE U.S. RETAINS THE CUP, IT'S THE GB&I'S SIDE BEST SHOWING IN AMERICA.

THE HAWK PULLS NO PUNCHES

During the pre-match dinner at the 1967 Ryder Cup, U.S. captain Ben Hogan completes the customary introductions of his team and announces: "Ladies and gentlemen, the United States Ryder Cup team—the finest golfers in the world." The next day, his team—which, again, did not include Jack Nicklaus—began a march to the most commanding victory in match history. The Americans routed the Great Britain team, 23½–8½.

SHORT-HANDED, BUT STILL STRONG

Despite the last-minute withdrawals of Hubert Green and Robert Barbarossa—so last-minute, in fact, that their names had been printed in the pre-match program—the United States secures its 20th Walker Cup victory at the 1969 matches.

SOMETHING NEW IN ST. LOUIS

Each side at the 1971 Ryder Cup featured three rookies and the United States team was further hindered by injuries to Lee Trevino and Billy Casper. Trevino, enjoying the best year of his career but slowed by appendectomy surgery a few weeks earlier, was nearly flawless, going 4–1 to help lead the Americans to an 18½–13½ victory at Old Warson Country Club in St. Louis, Missouri.

OLD COURSE UPSET

AT THE HALLOWED HOME OF GOLF, GREAT BRITAIN & IRELAND PULLS OFF A 13–11 UPSET OVER THE AMERICAN SIDE AT THE 1971 WALKER CUP. THE VICTORY IS GB&I'S FIRST SINCE THE 1938 MATCH, WHICH WAS ALSO PLAYED ON THE OLD COURSE AT ST. ANDREWS.

FOOD FOR THOUGHT

Locked in an 8–8 tie after two days at the 1973 Ryder Cup, Great Britain & Ireland's bid for victory gets off to a bad start when team leader Bernard Gallacher is sidelined with food poisoning on the eve of the singles matches. Peter Butler replaces Gallacher and records the first hole-in-one in match history, but it isn't enough to stem the U.S. onslaught. America wins or halves 13 of 16 singles matches to retain the Cup, 19–13.

CAMPBELL'S GOOD

At the 1975 matches, Bill Campbell, 52, finishes a Walker Cup career that spans three decades and includes a near-perfect 7–0–1 record in singles play. Fittingly, Campbell—who played his first Walker Cup for the United States in 1951— closes his career with a 2-and-1 victory over G. R. D. Eyles. Campbell served as playing captain at the 1955 matches and would later become the third American elected captain of the Royal and Ancient Golf Club of St. Andrews in 1987.

CONTINENTAL APPEAL

During the 1977 Ryder Cup—which was won by the United States, marking the team's 20th consecutive victory—officials from the PGA of America and Great Britain's PGA consider a proposal that would allow players from continental Europe to play on the GB&I team. Jack Nicklaus even makes his own impassioned pitch for the Europeans during the meeting and the measure is approved.

The old college try

U.S. Walker Cup teams have become little more than stepping stones to the professional ranks for American collegians by the time the 1979 matches are held at Muirfield, Scotland. The trend disturbs some so much, that the 1979 matches are scheduled at the same time as the NCAA Championship. The timing forces top amateurs John Cook, who is the reigning U.S. Amateur champion, Gary Hallberg, and Bobby Clampett to miss the event. Even without its top collegians, however, the U.S. drills GB&I, 15½–8½.

CLOSING THE GAP

In the first Ryder Cup that includes players from continental Europe, the United States needs a final-day singles boost to retain the Cup in 1979. Larry Nelson goes a perfect 5–0 to lead the United States to a 17–11 victory. The 1979 matches are the first to use the "envelope," a process where each captain inserts a name of a player in a sealed envelope in the event either team loses a player to injury. In the event of an injury, the "envelope" player sits out and the match he would have played in is considered tied.

HISTORY REPEATS AT HOYLAKE

For the first time since 1921, the Walker Cup returns to Royal Liverpool in Hoylake, England, for the 1983 matches. Hoylake was host of the first unofficial match between the United States and GB&I. The result is familiar. Like it did in 1921, the U.S. marches to victory in 1983.

WADKINS AVERTS AMERICAN COUP

Trailing by one hole with one hole to play, Lanny Wadkins hits his approach on the final hole to a foot for a birdie that halves his match with Jose Maria Canizares and secures a slim American victory at the 1983 Ryder Cup. The final outcome, 14½–13½, is the slimmest ever on American soil.

CLOSE CALL

THE UNITED STATES NIPS GREAT BRITAIN & IRELAND BY A SINGLE POINT TO WIN THE 1984 CURTIS CUP AT MUIRFIELD IN SCOTLAND. IT'S THE CLOSEST MATCH SINCE THE 1958 TIE IN MASSACHUSETTS.

Captain's club

U.S. playing captain Jay Sigel has a bit more than the normal home-soil advantage when the 1985 Walker Cup visits Pine Valley Golf Club in New Jersey. Sigel is the 1985 Pine Valley Club champion and leads the U.S. to a 13–11 victory. The matches mark the last time the storied layout hosts a USGA event.

EUROPEAN VACATION

With Tom Watson and Jack Nicklaus failing to qualify for the United States team, the Europeans turn the tide at the 1985 Ryder Cup. The momentum swings in the Europeans favor on day 2 when Craig Stadler misses a 3-footer on the final hole to halve his foursomes match. The Europeans complete the upset with seven singles victories for a 16½–11½ triumph.

AT HOME, ON THE PRAIRIE

Great Britain & Ireland stuns the United States at the 1986 Curtis Cup, routing the Americans 13–5 at Prairie Dunes Country Club in Kansas. It's GB&I's first victory in the United States and the team's first triumph since 1956.

Spanish conquest

Led by the Spanish duo of Seve Ballesteros and José María Olazábal, who went 3–1 in foursomes and four-ball play, the Europeans stun the Americans with their first victory on American soil at the 1987 Ryder Cup. The Europeans set the pace with a sweep of the afternoon four-ball matches on day 1, and close out the victory when Ireland's Eamonn Darcy nips Ben Crenshaw, 1 up, in singles.

GB&I'S GEORGIA PEACH

THE UNITED STATES' HOLD ON ALL OF GOLF'S CUPS (RYDER, CURTIS, AND WALKER) CONTINUES TO SLIP WHEN THE GREAT BRITAIN & IRELAND TEAM TURNS BACK THE UNITED STATES AT THE 1989 WALKER CUP AT PEACHTREE GOLF CLUB IN ATLANTA, GEORGIA. THE VICTORY IS GB&I'S FIRST ON U.S. SOIL.

A TIE THAT BINDS

For only the second time in its history, the 1989 Ryder Cup ends in a tie (14–14), which allows the Europeans to retain the trophy. Like they did in 1987, the Europeans build a lead during the first two days of team play and hold off an American singles' charge.

LADIES ONLY

A team of top female professionals from the United States routs their European counterparts at the maiden Solheim Cup, 11½–4½, in 1990 at Lake Nona in Orlando, Florida.

THE "WAR BY THE SHORE"

In a prelude to the heated affairs the matches would become, the 1991 Ryder Cup at The Ocean Course in South Carolina is dubbed the "War by the Shore." In hindsight, it was more of a battle of attrition. The teams were tied after two days, 8–8, and the Cup came down to the last match when Bernhard Langer missed his 6-foot par putt on the final hole to assure a 14½–13½ U.S. victory. Years later, European player David Feherty wrote about the ebb and flow of the 1991 matches: "It was like watching a train wreck: No one could look away . . . Despite everything—histrionics, over-the-top patriotism, blatant displays of bad taste—the golf had been outstanding."

Irish Eyes

Portmarnock Golf Club becomes the first course in Ireland to host the Walker Cup when the 1991 matches visit the seaside links. Yet the inspired venue does little to stop a determined U.S. team. Led by left-handed phenom Phil Mickelson, the U.S. cruises to a four-point victory and reclaims the Cup.

WORLD BEATERS

Fred Couples and Davis Love III both birdie the last hole of the 1992 World Cup to give the U.S. duo a one-stroke victory.

ONE BAD WEEK FOR THE U.S.

The 1992 Solheim Cup gets off to a rocky start for the Americans. U.S. captain Kathy Whitworth has to leave before the competition because of a family emergency. Things don't get any better for the United States in the matches, as the Europeans roll to an 11½–6½ victory.

SOMETHING OLD, SOMETHING NEW

An old American warhorse and a Ryder Cup rookie help the U.S. team to its most decisive victory, 15–13, in 13 years at the 1993 matches. At 51 years old, Raymond Floyd becomes the oldest Ryder Cup competitor and helps seal the U.S. victory with a 2-up triumph over European stalwart José María Olazábal. Cup rookie Davis Love III also spurs the rally with a 1-up decision over Constantino Rocca.

Generation gap

The average age of the U.S. Walker Cup team in 1993 is 31, compared to a GB&I average of 21. At 49, Jay Sigel is the U.S. squad's elder statesman, playing in his ninth consecutive match. In his last match, Sigel easily wins his final-day singles duel to lift the U.S. to a commanding 19–5 walkover. In 1993, Sigel turns pro and joins the Senior PGA Tour.

PRESIDENTS PREROGATIVE

The first Presidents Cup is played in 1994 at Robert Trent Jones Golf Club in Virginia. The matches are modeled after the Ryder Cup, but feature a team from the United States playing a group of international players from everywhere except Europe. The Americans win, 20–12, on the strength of the team's domination of singles play.

LIVING SINGLE

After building a two-point cushion heading into singles play, the host U.S. team is stunned by a final-day European rally at the 1995 Ryder Cup led by little-known Philip Walton and Howard Clark. Walton and Clark beat American heavyweights Jay Haas and Peter Jacobsen, respectively, in singles play to spark a 14½–13½ victory. The European comeback is the first time the United States has lost the singles portion of the competition since 1985.

TIGER CAN'T TURN GB&I TIDE

The pre-tournament hype of Tiger Woods's first, and only, Walker Cup appearance reaches new heights prior to the 1995 matches. Many view Woods as the game's next emerging superstar, but at Royal Porthcawl Golf Club, he goes a pedestrian 2–2 and GB&I steals the spotlight with a 14–10 upset.

Fearless Freddie

For the second consecutive match, Fred Couples clinches the trophy for the United States at the 1996 Presidents Cup. Couples—who birdied the 18th hole in his match with Nick Price to earn the winning point in the inaugural Cup two years earlier—holes a 30-foot birdie putt on the 17th hole of his singles match to deny Vijay Singh and secure a slim, 16½–15½, U.S. victory.

EUROPEAN ENIGMA

The U.S. rout of GB&I at the 1997 Walker Cup, 18–6, fuels a growing debate that would make amateurs from continental Europe eligible for the GB&I team. Many contend, after the blowout at Quaker Ridge Golf Club in New York, that expanding the Ryder Cup to include Europeans in 1979 made the matches more competitive and fueled the event's rise in popularity.

PAIN IN SPAIN

In the first Ryder Cup held outside the United States and Great Britain, the European side builds a 10½–5½ advantage at the 1997 matches and holds off the Americans in singles play for a one-point victory. The biggest disappointment for the U.S. is the play of Masters champion Tiger Woods, PGA winner Davis Love III, and British Open winner Justin Leonard—who struggle to a combined 1–9–3 record.

CLOSING THE DOOR DOWN UNDER

A lethargic U.S. team travels to Royal Melbourne in Australia for the 1998 Presidents Cup and suffers the worst loss in match history. Led by Shigeki Maruyama, Japan's "Smiling Assassin" who went a perfect 5–0 in his first Presidents Cup, the Internationals rout the Americans, 20½–11½. "We came to believe it was possible for us to beat an American team on American soil," said International captain Peter Thomson.

Beauty and the Beast

Tom Lehman is labeled the "Beast of Brookline" and one of the greatest comebacks in Ryder Cup history is marred by a breach of etiquette. Trailing by four points entering the final day of the 1999 matches, the United States sweeps to victory in eight of the first nine singles matches. With momentum swinging in the Americans favor, Justin Leonard sinks a 45-foot birdie putt at No. 17 that ignites a celebration by U.S. players, caddies, and wives on the green. Leonard's opponent, José María Olazábal, still has a chance to win the match with a 25-footer of his own. The green is cleared but the air is not—and Olazábal misses his putt. Said European assistant captain Sam Torrance: "It's about the most disgusting thing I've ever seen. Tom Lehman calls himself a man of God. His behavior today has been disgusting."

NO STOPPING GB&I AT NAIRN

Nairn Golf Club in Scotland hosts its first Walker Cup in 1999 and considering the outcome—a 6-point GB&I victory—the R&A will likely add the charming links adjacent the Moray Firth to the event's permanent rotation. For GB&I, future professional stars Luke Donald and Paul Casey post perfect 4–0 records.

TRAGEDY FORCES SCHEDULE CHANGE

THE SEPTEMBER 11, 2001, TERRORIST ATTACKS ON NEW YORK CITY AND WASHINGTON, D.C., PROMPT OFFICIALS TO POSTPONE THE RYDER CUP FOR ONE YEAR.

BACK-TO-BACK FOR GB&I

For the first time, GB&I retains the Walker Cup with its second-consecutive 6-point trouncing of the United States at the 2001 matches. The U.S. team is loaded with mid-amateurs, but the GB&I side again receives a big boost from Luke Donald, who turns pro directly after the matches.

Grand dame makes grand exit

Life-long amateur Carol Semple Thompson leads the United States to a commanding victory at the 2002 Curtis Cup. Thompson—playing in her record 12th Curtis Cup—holes a 27-foot birdie putt from the fringe on No. 18 to defeat Vikki Laing, 1 up, in singles play and secure the victory.

SOUTH AFRICAN STANDOFF

With the matches tied, 17–17, Ernie Els and Tiger Woods begin the first sudden-death playoff in Presidents Cup history, in 2003 at Fancourt Hotel in South Africa. After three playoff holes, the matches remain tied and, with darkness engulfing the course, captains Jack Nicklaus and Gary Player reach a gentleman's agreement to share the Cup.

GANTON GALLANTRY

Great Britain & Ireland solidifies its dominance of the Walker Cup, downing the U.S. team 12½–11½ in 2003. Since 1989, GB&I has won five of eight matches, thanks mainly to Gary Wolstenholme's play. Wolstenholme's 2–2 showing at Ganton Golf Club in England, improves his record to a GB&I career-best 9–8.

RYDER ROLL-OVER

Although the matches have a more congenial tone, the Europeans pull no punches on the course. Even on home turf, Oakland Hills Country Club in Michigan, the United States stands little chance at the 2004 Ryder Cup. The U.S. falls behind on the first day and never threatens on its way to an 18½–9½ loss, its worst in 77 years. The victory is Europe's second consecutive, and its fourth in the last five meetings. "This whole team and also myself, we just live for this," said Spain's Sergio García.

FIRST-TIMER FORTUNES

Three rookies post a combined 8–3–2 record at the 2005 Solheim Cup to propel the United States to a spirited 15½–12½ victory. Nineteen-year-old Paula Creamer led the American newcomers with a 3–1–1 record that included a decisive 7-and-5 thumping of European stalwart Laura Davies.

Wild ride in Windy City

In what U.S. captain Bob Lewis calls, "the greatest Walker Cup that was ever played," the American side holds off a determined rally and denies GB&I its fourth consecutive victory at Chicago Golf Club in 2005. The 1-point American victory—secured by Jeff Overton at the final green—is the tightest race since the 1989 match, which was won by GB&I.

ONE FOR JACK

The United States caps an emotional year for captain Jack Nicklaus with a down-to-the-wire triumph at the 2005 Presidents Cup. Chris DiMarco seals the title for the U.S. with a curling 15-foot birdie putt at the final hole to down Stuart Appleby. The biggest news for the U.S., however, is the pairing of Tiger Woods with Jim Furyk. Woods, who was a pedestrian 0-for-6 in Ryder and Presidents Cup four-ball play—was undefeated (2–0–1) with Furyk at his side.

Swings of time

"My swing is so bad I look like a caveman killing his lunch."
Lee Trevino

TAYLOR'S BEST (FLAT) FOOT FORWARD

Of the three players that made up the Great Triumvirate, John H. Taylor's swing was widely considered the least imposing. The former caddie was a stocky man who played flat-footed. But what his short, brisk swing lacked in beauty, it made up for in accuracy. Accuracy which he used to win five British Open titles, the last coming in 1913.

Diegeling

Considered one of the best ball-strikers of his time, Leo Diegel cured a balky putting stroke with a unique style in which he let his arms hang akimbo. The elbows-out style is nicknamed "Diegeling," and requires a player to hunch forward over a putt. The forearms form a straight line, locked by the hands on the putter grip, and the left elbow points at the cup.

THE JOPLIN GHOST

It's a commonly held belief that great putters are born, not made. Horton Smith is a testament to this bromide. Nicknamed "The Joplin Ghost," Smith was one of the original natural putters. He won 32 PGA Tour events, primarily through his prowess on the greens.

A SWING OF STEEL

Byron Nelson was one of the first players of the new era to have purposefully fashioned a swing for a steel-shafted club. This technique became evident at the 1939 U.S. Open when Nelson forced a second 18-hole playoff against Craig Wood. On the fourth hole of the second playoff, Nelson holed his 1-iron approach shot for an eagle-2 to relinquish a commanding lead.

COMING UP SHORT

If there was a weakness in Byron Nelson's game entering the 1945 season it was all but impossible for his competition to see. Yet before he embarked on his historic 18-victory season, Nelson spent most of his time improving his short game.

Dirty work

Although hardly beset by the kind of results that would prompt someone to change their swing, in 1946, Ben Hogan commits to curing his uncontrollable hook. "I hate a hook. It nauseates me. I could vomit when I see one. It's like a rattlesnake in your pocket," Hogan said. Although he discovers the "secret" to curing this, he refuses to tell anyone what it is. Years later, in a *Life* magazine article, he gives specifics about his 1946 swing changes. However, his wife, Valerie, as well as the golf public, believe the only secret Hogan had was a penchant for hard work.

ALWAYS A LOCKE

South African Bobby Locke became one of the game's most renowned putters using an action he picked up from Walter Hagen. Locke would take the putter back on an inside line and hood the face of the club for more overspin. During one particularly torrid run, Locke one-putted nine greens on his way to victory at the 1948 Chicago Victory Open. He is credited for being the first player to utter the ubiquitous line: "You drive for show but putt for dough."

MERION MAGIC

Ben Hogan's 1-iron approach shot to the 18th hole at Merion Golf Club in 1950 was frozen in time by *Life* magazine photographer Hy Peskin and has become part of U.S. Open lore. Hogan's majestic shot, however, simply set up a tie that forced an 18-hole playoff, which Hogan won.

A SWINGING READ

ERNEST JONES'S CLASSIC INSTRUCTION BOOK *SWING THE CLUBHEAD* IS PUBLISHED IN 1952 BY DODD, MEAD AND CO.

NEARLY PERFECT

In bowling, 300 is a perfect game and in baseball great sluggers aspire to hit for the cycle (single, double, triple, and home run). At the 1959 Pensacola Open, Bob Rosburg almost pulled off golf's version of perfection. In Round 3, he needed just 19 putts to complete his third round.

ALL THE WRIGHT MOVES

Although Ben Hogan's swing is often cited as an example of the perfect action, Mickey Wright's simple action earned "The Hawk's" praise. Both Hogan and Byron Nelson labeled Wright's swing one of the best. Like Hogan, Wright was a perfectionist who spent countless hours honing her swing.

Dropping bombs

Diminutive Jerry Barber was one of the PGA Tour's shortest hitters in 1961 but he made up for his lack of power with a prolific putter. At the 1961 PGA Championship, Barber put on a putting clinic—holing putts from 20 feet (birdie), 40 feet (par), and 60 feet (birdie) on his last three holes to force a playoff with Don January. In extra holes, Barber's flat stick remains hot and he won the playoff, 67–68.

CAPTAIN HOOK

Although 1963 proves to be a stellar year for Jack Nicklaus, it could have been even better if not for a poorly timed miscue. He'd got away with one at the 72nd hole at Augusta National, making a fortunate par to win his first Masters after hooking his tee shot sharply into a muddy areas from which he was given a free drop. Four months later, however, at Royal Lytham & St. Annes, Nicklaus again hooks his drive on the final hole into a bunker. This time he makes bogey and loses the British Open.

MARILYNN HAS HER MOMENT

Ben Hogan's 1-iron approach at Merion Golf Club during the 1950 U.S. Open may be considered "The Shot," but Marilynn Smith's 3-iron approach shot to the final hole of the 1964 Titleholders Championships is equally impressive. Smith's shot stops a foot from the hole for birdie and her second consecutive victory at the event.

A modern marvel

In 1966, Jack Nicklaus emerges as the game's preeminent shotmaker. Using a left-to-right ball flight, or power fade, the Golden Bear overwhelms most courses of the era, winning the 1966 Masters and British Open and finishing third at the U.S. Open. It's Nicklaus's power, combined with a creative short game and renowned putting stroke, that gives him his edge over the competition. "I came along during an era where the game of golf was more of a stylish game, and I added power to the game," said Nicklaus. "I was probably the first player that played with real power and was successful. And I was able to play with finesse as well."

MASTER-FUL MISTAKE

Count Gay Brewer's 3-footer on the final hole of the 1966 Masters ranks as one of the most high-profile gaffes in the game. His attempt blew by the hole and he ballooned to a 78 in a playoff to lose to Jack Nicklaus.

CROSSING OVER

Prior to his shocking victory at the 1969 U.S. Open, Orville Moody was a long-hitting former U.S. Army sergeant with a balky putter. Moody's putting woes were so acute he started putting cross-handed, with his left hand low on the grip. At Champions Golf Club in 1969, the odd grip worked but that victory was Moody's only PGA Tour title.

"THE HAWK" IS WATCHING

How respected was Ben Hogan's knowledge of the golf swing? As a young man, two-time major winner Tony Jacklin would imagine "The Hawk" standing close by while he practiced. "I would practice on my own for hundreds of hours and in my mind Ben Hogan was always standing over my right shoulder making a critique of every shot," Jacklin said.

The Machine

Gene Littler was dubbed "The Machine" because of his smooth, repeatable swing. That consistent action enabled Littler to finish among the top 60 money winners on the PGA Tour in 25 of his 26 years on Tour.

Saved by one swing

Reeling after back-to-back bogeys at Nos. 14 and 15 during the final round of the 1972 PGA Championship at Oakland Hills Country Club in Michigan, Gary Player's title hopes seem to vanish when he pushes his drive at the 16th far right. From a difficult lie and with willow trees blocking his path to the hole, Player muscles a 9-iron over a pond to 4 feet. He birdies the hole and wins by two shots.

LOW ROAD

Tied with Seve Ballesteros through 70 holes at the 1984 British Open, Tom Watson's 2-iron approach shot into the 17th hole on the Old Course at St. Andrews bounds over the green, crosses the road, and comes to rest against an ancient stone wall. Watson punches his chip onto the green but misses his 30-foot par putt and finishes two shots behind Ballesteros. There have been no shortage of heartbreaks on the Old Course's 17th, but Watson's ranks as the most high profile.

Little Red Book

For six decades, longtime swing instructor Harvey Penick kept track of various swing thoughts in a small, red notebook. Other than Penick's son, Tinsley, no one had seen his collection of swing wisdom until he publishes *Harvey Penick's Little Red Book* in 1992. The book sells over a million copies to become one of the largest selling sports-related books of all time.

THE NATURAL

Moe Norman is nicknamed "Pipeline Moe" for his unorthodox yet effective swing. Although his résumé doesn't rival Ben Hogan's, primarily because he suffers from autism, Norman is considered one of the game's best ball strikers. His PGA Tour career is brief, and in 1992 he is hired by Jack Kuykendall, who models his teaching system called Natural Golf after Norman's technique.

MIND OVER MATTER

Along with swing coaches, many modern PGA Tour players also work with a sports psychologist. Most mental coaches focus on maintaining a player's positive outlook. But keeping their clients from thinking too much is almost as important. "[PGA Tour player] Camilo Villegas has so much talent he only needs to dumb it down and play caveman golf—see ball, hit ball," said sports psychologist Gio Valiante.

Bagmen

"Show up, shut up and keep up."
Caddie credo

A LEGENDARY LOOP

The first international golf match on record is played at Leith, Scotland, in 1682 between the Duke of York (James II) and George Patterson and an unidentified team from England. The Scots win the match but, more importantly, Andrew Dickson carries the Duke of York's clubs during the event, making him the first-ever known caddie.

"OLD DA'S" OTHER JOB

IN THE LATE 19TH CENTURY, LEGENDARY LOCAL CADDIE DAVID "OLD DA" ANDERSON MOONLIGHTS WITH A GINGER BEER STAND HE SETS UP ON THE NINTH HOLE OF THE OLD COURSE AT ST. ANDREWS.

TEXAS TWO-STEP

Born the same year (1912), Ben Hogan and Byron Nelson learn the game as caddies in Texas. When they are 15, the two tie for first place in a nine-hole caddie tournament at Glen Garden Country Club in Fort Worth, Texas. Nelson wins a nine-hole playoff by a stroke.

A YOUNG MAN'S GAME

Given the physical demands of caddying, it's little surprise most of the early loopers were young men. Francis Ouimet, one of the game's most famous caddies, hired 10-year-old Eddie Lowery to carry his bag on his way to his stunning 1913 U.S. Open victory.

Bing's beginnings

Although he made his mark on the world as a musician, Bing Crosby's first love was golf. The crooner started one of the PGA Tour's most successful events at Pebble Beach Golf Links in California and was a decent player, winning the 1926 U.S. Musicians Championship. Crosby's interest in the game began when he was a 12-year-old caddie in Tacoma, Washington.

CASHING IN

Prior to the 1929 Ryder Cup, 16-year-old Ernest Hargreaves persuades Walter Hagen to hire him for the week. The American great keeps Hargreaves on the bag for the British Open a few weeks later, and The Haig (Hagen) cruises to the Open title and presents Hargreaves with the entire $100 winner's check.

CADDIE LIABILITY

IN NOVEMBER 1932, A COURT RULES THAT A GOLFER IS NOT RESPONSIBLE FOR DAMAGES TO HIS OWN CADDIE DURING THE COURSE OF A ROUND, BUT HE IS LIABLE IF HE HITS ANOTHER PLAYER'S CADDIE.

Show up, speak up, and clean up

Caddies at the four courses on the Monterey Peninsula (Pebble Beach, Cypress Point, Del Monte, and Spyglass Hill) are strongly advised to improve their broken English and manners.

CADDIES CARRY WARTIME LOAD

During World War II, caddies at Carnoustie Golf Club in Scotland carry gas masks for themselves and their players in case of a German attack.

EVANS'S SCHOLARSHIP CHICK'S LEGACY

In 1939, Chick Evans ends a competitive golf career that spans four decades and includes 54 victories. Evans won the 1916 U.S. Amateur and U.S. Open, but his greatest accomplishment is the Chick Evans Caddie Scholarship. The scholarship is originally funded by Evans's winnings and in 1930 the Western Golf Association becomes the program's sponsor.

MARTIN'S MISCUE

During the third round of the 1946 U.S. Open, Byron Nelson's caddie, Eddie Martin, heads under the gallery ropes to search for his boss' tee shot on the 15th hole. He inadvertently kicks the ball. Nelson is assessed a two-stroke penalty, finishes tied with Lloyd Mangrum after 72 holes, and loses in an 18-hole playoff.

SOUTHERN COMFORT

Until the 1960s, the only professional caddies on the PGA Tour came from Augusta National Golf Club's caddie corps. Loopers would meet a caddie during the Masters and—after Augusta National closed for the summer in May—they'd spend the rest of the season bouncing from city to city and professional to professional.

A BOLT OUT OF THE BLUE

Tommy Bolt's temper is part of golf lore. At one tournament during the mid-1950s, Bolt—who was known to break an offending club after a bad shot—addressed his 200-yard approach shot and asked his caddie what the right club was. "A 7-iron, Mr. Bolt," the caddie said. "A 7-iron!" Bolt asked. "What makes you think I can get there with a 7-iron?" The caddie replied: "Because that's the only club you have left in the bag."

Seeing is believing

Unlike other tournaments, Augusta National Golf Club did not allow players to use their own caddies during the Masters Tournament until 1983. Club caddies had to be used prior to 1983, a practice that didn't seem to bother Gary Player in 1961. Player was in contention for his first Masters title when he arrived at the par-3 16th. The South African thought his birdie putt should be aimed at the left edge of the cup, but his caddie disagreed. "It's right edge. If you put it there and it doesn't go in, I'm working for free this week. And you know I can't afford that," the caddie said. Player took the caddie's advice, made the putt, and won his first green jacket.

King and his court

Arnold Palmer used a combination of three caddies during the course of his Hall of Fame career. With James "Tip" Anderson, "The King" won two British Opens and with Nathaniel "Ironman" Avery claimed four green jackets at Augusta National. "Ironman wasn't the greatest caddie. I'd be less than honest if I said he was," Palmer said. "But his understanding of what made me tick was perhaps instinctive and definitely profound." When he wasn't at Augusta National or in the United Kingdom, Palmer employed Ernest "Creamy" Carolan during the 1970s and '80s.

TIMELESS TANDEM

One of the game's most famous caddie-player tandems begins in a St. Louis, Missouri, parking lot in 1973. Tom Watson hires Bruce Edwards to caddie for him for a week, but their partnership endures for nearly four decades. In 2004, Edwards dies after an extended battle with Amyotrophic Lateral Sclerosis (Lou Gehrig's Disease).

THE BIG BANANA

Bruce Lietzke's ability to take time off without practicing and still remain competitive is legendary. In 1984, Lietzke took a 5½-month hiatus to be with his pregnant wife and won his third tournament back. Later that year, Lietzke hired a new caddie, who doubted his boss's lax work ethic. "I said, 'Man, I'm not touching these clubs until I see you at the Bob Hope tournament,' and that was I think 15 weeks. He didn't believe me," Lietzke said. To prove Lietzke didn't spend the entire off-season away from the range, the caddie slipped a banana under the headcover on Lietzke's driver. Fifteen weeks later at the duo's first event of 1985, the caddie was stunned to discover a moldy banana exactly where he left it. "I didn't know what he was doing," Lietzke said.

From caddie to champion

In 1986, Mark Calcavecchia loses his status on the PGA Tour and spends the week of the Honda Classic working as a caddie for Ken Green. A year later, Calcavecchia regains his Tour card and completes his comeback with a three-shot victory at the Honda.

SOMETHING TO THINK ABOUT

Chip Beck reaches the par-5 15th hole at Augusta National with a chance to catch front-runner Bernhard Langer at the 1993 Masters.

After a good drive, Beck has 235 yards to the green from the middle of the fairway, but after a lengthy debate with his caddie, Pete Bender, he decides to lay up on the hole and makes par. "I asked him why he didn't want to go for [the green in two shots]. He looked me straight in the face, and said, 'I don't want to mess my round up,'" Bender said. Beck finished four shots behind Langer, in second place.

Time for a change

Tiger Woods turns pro in 1996 and hires long-time PGA Tour caddie Mike "Fluff" Cowan. Through the duo's first 2½ years, Woods wins eight titles including the 1997 Masters. But in 1999, the two go through a high-profile split and Woods replaces Cowan with New Zealander Steve Williams.

WHAT'S IN A NAME?

More so than any other profession, caddying seems to encourage the use of nicknames. Among the more popular monikers among modern caddies are: Jeff ""Squeaky"" Medlin, Tony "Greasy" Navarro, Jim "Bones" Mackay, "Last Call" Lance Ten Broek (whose son, who is also a caddie, is nicknamed "First Call" and Ten Broek dubs his ex-wife "Collect Call"), Ron "Bambi" Levin, and "Penitentiary" Larry, a likable ex-con who prefers not to give out his last name.

One wrong makes a right

Three under par through three holes at the 1995 San Jose Open, professional journeyman John Maginnes steps to the fourth tee and asks his long-time caddie for the yardage on the par-3 hole. The yardage Maginnes's man announces doesn't seem right so he asks him to calculate it again. "Where are we?" the caddie asks. "No. 4," Maginnes answers. "No, what course are we playing?" the caddie asks. Seems Maginnes's looper has the yardage book from another course. Despite the gaffe, Maginnes goes on to win the event.

CADDIE SLAM

Longtime PGA Tour bagman Dave Renwick caddies three different players to Grand Slam victories. The first comes in 1995 when he's on the bag for Steve Elkington's PGA Championship victory. He adds another PGA title (Vijay Singh, 1998) and three Masters triumphs (José María Olazábal, 1994 and '99; Singh 2000) to his résumé.

SHAKE DOWN

Carin Koch's caddie—who is her husband, Stephan—is accused by another caddie of shaking a tree to dislodge Koch's wayward tee shot during the third round of the 1997 LPGA Corning Classic. The Kochs deny the claim, but the following day she is assessed a two-stroke penalty after an elderly couple claim they saw Stephan Koch shake the tree.

Oh, brother!

Chris Heintz, brother of PGA Tour player Bob, may have one of the more interesting schedules for a caddie. Chris Heintz is a catcher with the Minnesota Twins and he plays for that team's Triple-A club for most of the summer. When he's not behind the plate, Chris Heintz caddies for his brother. The duo's most famous pairing was at the 1999 Shreveport Open, which Bob Heintz won thanks to some timely advice from his brother. "We were on the last hole and I wanted to hit 5-iron and he said, 'If you hit 5 [-iron], as excited as you are, you're going to kill someone.'"

ONE OF THEIR OWN

Greg Puga, a Hispanic caddie at posh Bel-Air Country Club in California, wins the 2000 U.S. Mid-Amateur to earn a spot in the 2001 Masters. Puga hires veteran Augusta National looper Joe Collins, who said it was as good as getting the bag of a potential Masters champion.

Tiger who?

Although well short of the contentious atmosphere surrounding recent Ryder Cups, the 2000 Presidents Cup features a touch of controversy. Vijay Singh's caddie, Paul Tesori, wears a hat with "Tiger who?" stitched into the back during the Fijian's singles match against Tiger Woods. Woods wins the match, 2 and 1, and leads the United States to a 21½–10½ victory.

THREE'S A CROWD

Some caddie/player relationships are a little more fiery than others. During the 2004 FedEx St. Jude Classic, Mathias Gronberg and his caddie get into an argument mid-way through the first round and the caddie drops the bag and walks off the course. Gronberg recruits a member of the small gallery following his group to take his caddie's place, but the temp can only go a few holes before he has to leave. A second member of the gallery is drafted into service and Gronberg completes his round. "He went through three caddies in one day. That's got to be a record," said Brandt Snedeker, one of Gronberg's playing partners.

PAYDAY

Caddies on the PGA Tour usually earn between 5–7 percent of their player's winnings plus a weekly stipend, which ranges from $500 to $1,000. That cut climbs to 10 percent for a victory, plus, if you have a particularly generous boss, whatever extras may be doled out. After winning the 2005 Ford Championship at Doral, for example, Tiger Woods gave his caddie, Steve Williams, the Ford sports car that came with the winner's check.

SIBLING SUPPORT

At the 2005 PGA Championship, teaching pro Ron Philo Jr. enlists the services of his sister, LPGA Tour standout Laura Diaz, for the week. The 90-degree heat and hilly Baltusrol Golf Club layout are demanding enough, but Diaz also has to contend with being four months pregnant. "He's going easy on me," Diaz said after the first round.

The rub of the green

"To praise me for that is to congratulate someone for not robbing a bank."
Bobby Jones after calling a penalty on himself

An honorable start

The original Rules of Golf were written in 1744 by the Gentleman Golfers of Leith—who were later renamed the Honorable Company of Edinburgh Golfers—and dealt principally with match-play competitions, not stroke or medal play, which is popular today.

A STROKE OF LUCK

STROKE OR MEDAL PLAY IS THE PREFERRED MODERN FORM OF COMPETITION, BUT THE EARLIEST REFERENCE TO STROKE PLAY AT ST. ANDREWS OCCURS AROUND 1759.

TIME OUT

For those who believe slow play is a recent phenomenon, consider Law XII of the Aberdonians' "Laws of the Game," which limits a search for a lost ball to five minutes. The rule, which was written by members of Royal Aberdeen Golf Club in 1783, is still strictly adhered to.

PLAYING THE BALL AS IT LIES

IN 1856, A RULE CHANGE IS ENACTED THAT STIPULATES THAT IN MATCH PLAY THE BALL MUST BE PLAYED AS IT LIES OR THE HOLE IS CONCEDED.

A round of 18

In 1858, the Old Course at St. Andrews decrees that "one round of the Links or 18 holes is reckoned a match unless otherwise stipulated." The new rule encourages other clubs to convert to or build to 18 holes in length. Why St. Andrews members pick 18 holes is not known, but one local tale has it that it takes exactly 18 shots to polish off a fifth of Scotch. One shot per hole seems about right.

AMATEUR STATUS

In August 1901, the U.S. Golf Association describes 13 reasons a golfer would forfeit amateur status. Included in that list is caddying after the age of 15 and competing professionally in any sport.

HANDICAPPING THE FIELD

In 1905, Leighton Calkin authors *A System for Club Handicapping,* which becomes the basis for the U.S. Golf Association's eligibility criteria into the U.S. Amateur. Six years later, the USGA sets the handicap limit to enter the U.S. Amateur at 6.

Growing pains

As golf's popularity in the United States grows in the early part of the 20th century, a debate arises over which organization—the U.S. Golf Association or the Western Golf Association—should be the game's sanctioning body. In 1909, the WGA considers changing its name to the "American Golf Association" to challenge the USGA's authority.

"NO FLUKES"

In 1911, the U.S. Golf Association loosely defines par as the number of strokes needed per hole for "perfect play without flukes and under ordinary weather conditions, always allowing two strokes on each putting green."

OUIMET'S DILEMMA

Francis Ouimet, by far the era's most accomplished amateur, opens a sporting goods business in 1916 despite a U.S. Golf Association rule that denies amateur status to any player who capitalizes on their fame to promote the sale of sporting goods. The dispute deepens the split between the USGA and the Western Golf Association, which threatens to form its own organization that would supplant the USGA as the nation's rulemaking body. Three years later, Ouimet's amateur status is reinstated and the WGA threat subsides.

ROYAL AND ANCIENT AUTHORITY

IN 1919, THE ROYAL AND ANCIENT GOLF CLUB OF ST. ANDREWS ASSUMES CONTROL OF THE BRITISH OPEN AND BRITISH AMATEUR CHAMPIONSHIPS.

Oceans apart

Rule debates between the U.S. Golf Association and the Royal and Ancient Golf Club are not new. In 1920, USGA president George Herbert Walker, grandfather of U.S. President George Bush and great grandfather of President George W. Bush, urges the R&A to standardize golf balls and outlaw the stymie, which occurs in match play when one player's ball blocks another's path to the hole. Neither issue is resolved.

Hutchison "ribbing"

Using a set of "ribbed" clubs that will soon become illegal, Jock Hutchison wins the 1921 British Open at St. Andrews. With the new clubs that give players extra spin on approach shots, Hutchison scores a hole-in-one in the first round, ties Roger Wethered at 296, and easily prevails in a 36-hole playoff (150–159).

STANDARD SPHERES

THE U.S. GOLF ASSOCIATION AND ROYAL AND ANCIENT GOLF CLUB AGREE TO A STANDARD-SIZED GOLF BALL FOR CHAMPIONSHIP PLAY OF 1.62 INCHES IN DIAMETER AND 1.62 OUNCES.

TESTING, 1-2-3

At a facility on Jekyll Island in Georgia, the U.S. Golf Association starts testing golf balls in 1924.

STEELY MOVE

The U.S. Golf Association moves into new offices in Manhattan in 1924 and also approves the use of steel-shafted golf clubs in all championships played after April 11 of that year.

RULES TO LIVE BY

Bobby Jones calls a penalty on himself when his ball moves as he addresses a putt during the 1926 British Open. Jones, who wins the championship by two strokes, is lauded for his actions, but he's mystified by the support. "To praise me for that is to congratulate someone for not robbing a bank," Jones said.

SOUTHERN DISCOMFORT

Joe Turnesa didn't win the 1927 Southern Open but his actions attracted the most attention. During the tournament, Turnesa's driver head flew off during his backswing. Even though he hadn't started his downswing, officials assessed Turnesa a one-stroke penalty.

QUEST FOR UNIFORMITY

IN AUGUST 1928, THE ROYAL AND ANCIENT GOLF CLUB UNVEILS ITS PLAN FOR A UNIFORM GOLF BALL. LIKE THE USGA'S VERSION, THE NEW LIMITS WILL BE 1.68 INCHES IN DIAMETER AND 1.55 OUNCES.

THRILLS AND GASPARILLA
Claiming the game "needs greater thrills," Gene Sarazen suggests the USGA use an 8-inch (in diameter) cup on the greens. Shortly after his request, officials at the 1933 Gasparilla Open in Tampa, Florida, put the 8-inch cup in play.

USGA: DIDRIKSON NO AMATEUR
The U.S. Golf Association in 1935 rules that Mildred "Babe" Didrikson, a former U.S. Olympic track and field star, is ineligible to compete in any amateur events because of her activities as a professional baseball player.

STYMIED
The Massachusetts Golf Association becomes one of the first organizations to drop the stymie rule in 1936. Bowing to pressure from players, the USGA modifies the stymie rule in 1938 to allow a ball within 6 inches of another and within 6 inches of the hole to be lifted until the other golfer has played their shot. The same year, the USGA also institutes a rule limiting a player to 14 clubs. Some contend, the "14 club" rule is in reaction to Lawson Little's practice of arriving at events with up to 30 clubs in his bag.

EARLY RISER

Ed Oliver finishes 72 holes tied for the lead at the 1940 U.S. Open but is disqualified for having teed off before his scheduled starting time in the final round. Oliver, along with five other players who were also disqualified, teed off early in an attempt to beat an approaching storm.

Bookworm

Australian amateur Jim Ferrier is deemed ineligible for the 1940 U.S. Amateur by the USGA because reportedly he had been paid to write a book on golf instruction.

IN THE GROOVE

The USGA sets new standards for grooves in golf clubs in 1940. The rule states grooves can be no wider than $\frac{1}{32}$ of an inch and the distance between grooves can be no less than three times the width of the groove.

"BABE" BACK IN THE FOLD

IN EARLY 1944, THE USGA REINSTATES BABE DIDRIKSON'S AMATEUR STATUS. THE ORGANIZATION RULED THE FORMER U.S. OLYMPIC TRACK AND FIELD STAR INELIGIBLE IN 1935 BECAUSE SHE WAS A PROFESSIONAL BASEBALL PLAYER.

TUFTS CUSTOMER

Richard Tufts, owner of Pinehurst Resort in North Carolina and chairman of the USGA's Handicap Committee, leads the charge in 1947 to revise the Rules of Golf. Under Tufts's leadership, the rules are simplified and cut from 61 to 21. Although the Royal and Ancient Golf Club initially rejects the amendments, a unification of the Rules by the USGA and R&A occurs in 1951.

AS A RULE
The PGA Tour agrees before the 1948 season to conduct its championships according to USGA rules.

GENDER GAP

After Babe Zaharias announces her plans to play the 1948 U.S. Open, the USGA rules that women will not be allowed to compete in the championship.

Stymie solution

After years of debate, the USGA and R&A agree to outlaw the stymie, starting in 1952. Other rule changes include the legalization of center-shafted putters and a greater penalty for shots hit out-of-bounds. A player will have to take a stroke and distance penalty, which means playing a second ball from the spot of the original shot, for wayward shots.

SAVE THE LAST DANCE

So excited is Hawaii's Jackie Pung by her victory at the 1952 U.S. Women's Amateur Championship that she breaks into a victory hula before being asked by USGA officials to refrain from dancing.

Bending the rules

In his foursomes match with Gene Littler at the 1953 Walker Cup, Jimmy Jackson discovers after two holes that he is playing with 16 clubs in his bag, two over the legal limit. Initially, the two Americans are disqualified as prescribed by the rules. But after Great Britain & Ireland captain Tony Duncan pleads with officials on the Americans' behalf, the ruling is reversed and the match continues with the Americans receiving a two-hole penalty. "This is ridiculous. We haven't come 3,000 miles to win a 36-hole match by default on the second hole," Duncan said. The Americans recover from the incident, and win the match, 3 and 2.

SHORT TAKE

In 1954, the USGA approves the wearing of shorts by female competitors in its championships.

A FINE FIGHT

Although the Rules of Golf don't cover physical altercations between competitors, the PGA Tour takes a dim view of this type of behavior. At the 1954 Greater Greensboro Open, Doug Ford and Bill Nary are fined by the Tour after nearly coming to blows.

THE USGA'S LONGSHOT

In an attempt to stop the practice of high-stakes Calcuttas (or wagers), the USGA enacts an anti-gambling clause into the Rules of Amateur Status.

CRIME AND PUNISHMENT

Harvie Ward is considered the best amateur since Bobby Jones during the 1950s. He'd won two U.S. Amateurs and the 1952 British Amateur, but in 1957, Ward's employer, Edward E. Lowery, testifies that he paid Ward's expenses in two events. The payment is a clear violation of the Rules of Amateur Status, and the USGA strips Ward of his amateur status for one year.

WRIGHT IS WRONG

Mickey Wright shoots a woeful 104 in the opening round of the 1957 Tampa Women's Open after being penalized 24 strokes for having an extra club in her bag for 12 holes.

A KING'S CORRECTION

Arnold Palmer is one-shot clear of the field and closing on his first green jacket during the final round of the 1958 Masters when his tee shot at the par-3 12th finishes plugged in its own pitch mark. Although initially denied relief by an official, Palmer plays two balls—the embedded ball, which he makes a double bogey with, and another that is dropped out of the pitch mark, which he pars. Before finishing his round, Palmer is informed he was allowed relief and is given a par on the 12th. He wins by one shot.

Living single

The USGA trashes its dual-handicap system—which allows players to keep a "current" as well as a "basic" handicap—in favor of a single-handicap model, beginning in 1958.

MEMBERS ONLY

THE PGA TOUR OFFICIALLY DROPS THE "CAUCASIANS-ONLY" CLAUSE FROM ITS CONSTITUTION IN 1961, ALLOWING AFRICAN-AMERICANS TO BECOME MEMBERS.

CASUAL CONTENDER

*Officials grant Jack Nicklaus a free drop out
of casual water on the final hole of the 1963
Masters. Nicklaus makes par on the hole and,
at 23, becomes the event's youngest champion.*

Time's up

In 1964, the USGA adopts a rule
limiting the amount of time a player can
wait for a ball hanging on the lip of the
hole to drop. A year later, Tommy Bolt is
the first player penalized under the new
10-second rule during the second round
of the Colonial National Invitational.

A BIG HIT

The USGA scraps a rule that penalizes players
who hit a flagstick from off the green. A ball hit
from off the putting surface, but within 20 yards
of the hole, can now strike an unattended flagstick
without penalty.

COSTLY MISCUE FOR WHITWORTH

CAROL MANN WINS THE 1966 RALEIGH LADIES
INVITATIONAL BY ONE SHOT WHEN KATHY WHITWORTH
CALLS A TWO-STROKE PENALTY ON HERSELF ON THE
FINAL HOLE.

FATHER KNOWS BEST

Jack Klass challenges an LPGA rule that requires that players be at least 18 years old. Klass's $1.25 million lawsuit is intended to open the door for his 10-year-old daughter, Beverly, who played three LPGA events in 1967. In July, a judge dismisses the lawsuit.

"What a stupid I am"

Reigning British Open champion Roberto De Vicenzo finishes tied with Bob Goalby at 11 under at the 1968 Masters. However, he must adjust his score when officials learn that De Vicenzo's playing partner, Tommy Aaron, mistakenly wrote down a par-4 on No. 17 instead of the Argentine's correct score— birdie-3. Since he'd signed his scorecard, De Vicenzo had to settle for the higher score and finishes a shot behind Goalby. De Vicenzo blamed himself, not Aaron, for the mistake. "What a stupid I am," he said.

PGA PROBLEMS

An ongoing battle between Tour players and the PGA of America is temporarily settled in 1968 when the PGA forms the Tournament Players Division. Earlier in the year, some players bolted the PGA to form their own circuit, the short-lived American Professional Golfers.

THE CONCESSION

Only in match play is a player allowed to concede another player's putt. The most famous occurrence of this was at the 1969 Ryder Cup in England. With the matches tied, Jack Nicklaus missed a birdie putt on the last hole that would have given him a 1-up victory over Tony Jacklin and the United States a slim triumph. Before Jacklin had a chance to officially square the match with his par putt, Nicklaus conceded the 2-footer. "I don't think you would have missed that, Tony, but under the circumstances I'd never give you the opportunity," Nicklaus said. It's the first time in Ryder Cup history the matches finished in a tie.

Blalock blue after Bluegrass disqualification

Jane Blalock is disqualified from the 1972 Bluegrass Invitational after other players accuse her of cheating by moving her golf ball on the green. Shortly after her disqualification, the LPGA suspends Blalock through 1979. Blalock challenges the suspension and is granted an injunction by a federal judge.

SETTING A STANDARD

The USGA sets an overall distance standard for golf balls. Beginning in 1976, future golf balls must not exceed an average of 280 yards when driven by a mechanical golfer under standard test conditions.

Extra hole overhaul

In 1976, the Masters announces it will go to a sudden-death playoff, instead of an 18-hole playoff, in the case of a tie. The next year, the PGA also switches to the sudden-death format.

THE FIX IS NOT IN

In early 1978, the USGA considers a rule to ban golf balls that correct a player's slice or hook in flight.

ONE FOR ALL

The PGA Tour adopts the "one-ball rule" in 1979, which requires competitors to play a single brand and type of golf ball for an entire round. Prior to the "one-ball rule," players regularly switch from a wound ball to a two-piece ball in order to gain an advantage on certain shots.

THE AGE OF PALMER

The USGA reduces the minimum age requirement for the 1981 U.S. Senior Open from 55 to 50 to allow crowd-favorite Arnold Palmer to play. Palmer, 51, finishes tied with Billy Casper and Bob Stone at 289 and wins the playoff.

UNDER HIS SKIN

The Skins Game debuts in 1983 on NBC with four of the era's top players—Gary Player, Jack Nicklaus, Tom Watson, and Arnold Palmer. Player wins the event with $170,000, but afterward Watson and the "Black Knight" get into a heated discussion over a possible rule violation. Watson claims Player moved a leaf near his ball before chipping onto the 16th green. Player denies the violation.

BEAN COUNTER

Andy Bean is penalized two strokes for putting with the handle of his putter during the third round of the 1983 Canadian Open.

DOUBLE HIT DOOMS CHEN

Leading the 1985 U.S. Open with 14 holes to play, T.C. Chen unintentionally double hits his chip on the fifth hole at Oakland Hills Country Club in Michigan. Chen makes double bogey on the hole to blow a four-stroke lead and lose the championship. He's also saddled with the moniker "Two-Chip Chen" for the rest of his career.

MAKING A POINT

A unique form of scoring debuts at the 1986 International in Colorado. The event uses a modified Stableford format that awards players 8 points for double eagle, 5 for eagle, 2 for birdie, 0 for par, −1 for bogey, and −3 for double bogey or higher.

Anger management

Clubs broken during the "normal course of play" can be replaced. However, clubs damaged out of anger are not replaceable, nor can a player continue to use the damaged club. During the 1987 Ryder Cup, Ben Crenshaw slams his putter against his foot, breaking the shaft. He finishes the match, which he loses, putting with a 1-iron.

REPTILE RULING

One of the most under-used rules of golf is the "rule of equity." It is, essentially, a catch-all rule that allows for a fair solution to an unforeseeable situation. An example occurs at the 1988 Bay Hill Invitational, when Tim Simpson's tee shot during the third round stops just short of a water hazard but within feet of a 10-foot alligator. Simpson is allowed to drop a new ball, away from the alligator, without penalty.

Blue day at Blue Monster

During the first round of the 1991 Doral Ryder Open, Paul Azinger hits his drive into the lake adjacent the 18th fairway on Doral's famous "Blue Monster" layout. Azinger chips the partially submerged ball back to the fairway, but while he's taking his stance his left foot moves a rock in the water. The next day, after a second-round 65 had put him within a shot of the lead, officials inform him he has been disqualified for moving an object in a hazard. A television viewer had watched the event and called Tour officials, who confirm Azinger had moved the rock. Because he's already signed his scorecard, Azinger is disqualified.

SLIPPERY SLOPE

In March 1991, the USGA moves the entire country under the slope system for USGA handicaps. The new slope rating—which can range from 55 to 155, with 113 being a layout of average difficulty—represents the relative difficulty of a course for bogey golfers compared to its course rating.

AN AMATEUR NO MORE

While attending the University of Alabama on a golf scholarship in 1992, Jason Bohn enters a hole-in-one contest during a charity event and scores an improbable ace worth $1 million. Bohn is forced to give up his amateur status, and his scholarship to Alabama, to accept the prize. Each October through 2012, Bohn receives a $50,000 check for the hole-in-one, which probably eases the blow for a shortened amateur career.

RIGHT BALL, WRONG MARK

Greg Norman is disqualified from the 1996 Greater Hartford Open for playing with a non-conforming golf ball. Although the ball Norman uses is conforming, the side stamp on the ball has not been approved by the USGA.

TICKET TO RIDE

Oregon pro Casey Martin, who suffers from a debilitating circulatory ailment that makes it difficult for him to walk, qualifies for the 1998 U.S. Open, and the USGA allows him to use a golf cart during the championship. Later that year, Martin wins a federal lawsuit against the PGA Tour, giving him the right to use a cart in Tour-sanctioned events.

A SIMPLE RULE

The original Rules of Golf have not changed much since the Honorable Company of Edinburgh Golfers put them to paper in 1744. Today, there are only 34 rules in golf, fewer than baseball, basketball, football, soccer, rugby, and cricket.

HEAVY LIFTING

During the 1999 Phoenix Open, Tiger Woods's tee shot on the 13th hole during the final round comes to rest behind a boulder in a natural area. A Tour rules official deems the 1,000-pound boulder a loose impediment which isn't "solidly embedded" and, with the help of about a dozen men in the gallery, Woods is allowed to move the obstruction.

THE "SAM SNEAD" RULE

Sam Snead cured an often-faulty putter by facing the hole when he putted and using a croquet-style stroke, an action the USGA quickly outlawed. In 1999, at the U.S. Senior Open, Arnold Palmer is penalized two-strokes for putting "astride" the hole.

TAKING TURNS

Clinging to a 1-up lead during the 2000 Solheim Cup, the U.S. tandem of Kelly Robbins and Pat Hurst appears to fall into a tie with the European team of Annika Sörenstam and Janice Moodie when Sörenstam chips in for birdie at the 12th hole. But Sörenstam is forced to replay the shot when it's learned she played out of turn. The Swede doesn't chip in the second time, and the Europeans lose the match, 2 and 1.

Splash sinks Russell

After marking his ball on the 17th green during play at the 2001 English Open, Raymond Russell tosses the orb to his caddie who misses the throw and allows the ball to drop into a water hazard. Russell is unable to find the ball in the pond and is saddled with a two-stroke penalty for finishing the hole with the wrong ball.

One too many

The rule limiting players to 14 clubs has been broken often since its inception in 1938 by the USGA. Yet few violations of the rule have been as public as Ian Woosnam's blunder at the 2001 British Open. The Welshman began the final round among the leaders but discovered on the second hole his caddie had failed to remove a driver he'd been testing from his bag on the practice range before the round. The ensuing two-stroke penalty cost Woosnam a shot at the title. "At that moment, I felt like I had been kicked in the teeth," said Woosnam.

LOCAL RULES

While the Rules of Golf cover most general occurrences, specific local rules abound depending on the region and the golf course. Overhead power lines at La Costa Resort in California come into play on numerous holes. If a player clips the lines with a shot, "the stroke shall be canceled and must be replayed without penalty." The most famous local rule involves the notorious 17th hole at the Old Course in St. Andrews. Unlike roads or cart paths on other courses, which are considered out of play, the tarmac that runs adjacent the 17th green is part of the course. Shots that come to rest on the road or against a centuries-old stone wall behind the green must be played as they lie.

LEGAL LASER
THE USGA AND R&A AGREE IN 2005 TO ALLOW LASER DISTANCE-MEASURING DEVICES IN COMPETITIONS. THE DECISION REPRESENTS, AT LEAST IN PART, AN ATTEMPT TO SPEED UP PLAY.

DISASTROUS DEBUT
In her much-anticipated professional debut, teenage phenom Michelle Wie takes a penalty drop for an unplayable lie during the third round of the 2005 LPGA Samsung World Championship. A reporter for Sports Illustrated *watches the incident and concludes Wie dropped closer to the hole than where the ball originally lay, a violation of the rules. The reporter doesn't inform officials of the incident until the next day. Wie is disqualified for signing an incorrect scorecard.*

PLAYERS INDEX

THE GOLF GEEK'S BIBLE

THE GOLF GEEK'S BIBLE